PUBLIC HEALTH IN THE 21ST CENTURY

ADHERENCE TO TREATMENT IN CLINICAL PRACTICE

PUBLIC HEALTH IN THE 21ST CENTURY

Additional books in this series can be found on Nova's website under the Series tab.

Additional e-books in this series can be found on Nova's website under the e-book tab.

Public Health in the 21st Century

Adherence to Treatment in Clinical Practice

Pamela Lofland
Editor

New York

Copyright © 2014 by Nova Science Publishers, Inc.

All rights reserved. No part of this book may be reproduced, stored in a retrieval system or transmitted in any form or by any means: electronic, electrostatic, magnetic, tape, mechanical photocopying, recording or otherwise without the written permission of the Publisher.

For permission to use material from this book please contact us:
Telephone 631-231-7269; Fax 631-231-8175
Web Site: http://www.novapublishers.com

NOTICE TO THE READER

The Publisher has taken reasonable care in the preparation of this book, but makes no expressed or implied warranty of any kind and assumes no responsibility for any errors or omissions. No liability is assumed for incidental or consequential damages in connection with or arising out of information contained in this book. The Publisher shall not be liable for any special, consequential, or exemplary damages resulting, in whole or in part, from the readers' use of, or reliance upon, this material. Any parts of this book based on government reports are so indicated and copyright is claimed for those parts to the extent applicable to compilations of such works.

Independent verification should be sought for any data, advice or recommendations contained in this book. In addition, no responsibility is assumed by the publisher for any injury and/or damage to persons or property arising from any methods, products, instructions, ideas or otherwise contained in this publication.

This publication is designed to provide accurate and authoritative information with regard to the subject matter covered herein. It is sold with the clear understanding that the Publisher is not engaged in rendering legal or any other professional services. If legal or any other expert assistance is required, the services of a competent person should be sought. FROM A DECLARATION OF PARTICIPANTS JOINTLY ADOPTED BY A COMMITTEE OF THE AMERICAN BAR ASSOCIATION AND A COMMITTEE OF PUBLISHERS.

Additional color graphics may be available in the e-book version of this book.

Library of Congress Cataloging-in-Publication Data

ISBN: 978-1-63117-841-2

Published by Nova Science Publishers, Inc. † New York

CONTENTS

Preface		vii
Chapter 1	Clinical Treatment Outcomes *Kathy Sexton-Radek*	1
Chapter 2	Theoretical Models of Adherence *Sara Garfield*	19
Chapter 3	Clinical Implications of Adherence to Treatment of Patients with Social Anxiety *Mariângela Gentil Savoia and Silvia Sztamfater*	31
Chapter 4	Motivation and Adherence in Management of Chronic Pain *Zlatka Rakovec-Felser*	49
Index		85

PREFACE

Traditionally, medical adherence has been viewed as the extent to which a patient follows a prescriber's instructions. Adherence to treatment is a relevant factor able to influence results obtained by clinical trials and clinical practice. The components of adherence can be considered by the actions of patients, professionals, family and social support programs. Concerning mental health disorders, nonadherence is related to poorer treatment outcomes, such as lack of symptom stabilization, homelessness, lower quality of life and hospitalization. This book discusses clinical treatment outcomes, along with the clinical implications adherence has on patients with social anxiety, and chronic pain. It also provides several theoretical models of adherence.

Chapter 1 – The literature that examines adherence to treatment is represented in this chapter. Adherence to medical regimens and medication has been predominantly represented in this literature base. However, Behavioral interventions are described in terms of mental health treatments and psychoeducational approaches have also been included in this literature. The methodology predominantly, in a majority of the investigations, was survey based with random treatment control used for outcome measures of medication adherence. Treatment adherence is commonly referenced to these medication adherence studies. Some conclusions are presented for the reader. It is concluded from the findings in this area, that mild levels of adherence to treatment exists.

Chapter 2 – In this chapter theoretical models of adherence to medical treatment are reviewed. The chapter begins by describing the traditional biomedical approach and then moves on to explain the broader psychological approaches including: the health belief model, health locus of control theory, self efficacy theory, the theory of planned behaviour, the self-regulatory model and the transtheroetical stages of change model. The limitations of these psychological models are discussed and a more contemporary view of adherence using the accident causation framework is described. Finally, a move away from only focussing on adherence to incorporating other concepts such as shared decision making is described. For each model, the effects of the theoretical approach on the types of interventions that are employed to monitor and reduce non –adherence to treatment are discussed.

Chapter 3 – *Background:* Adherence to treatment is a relevant factor able to influence results obtained by clinical trials and clinical practice. The components of adherence can be considered by the actions of patients, professionals, family and social support programs. Concerning mental health disorders, nonadherence is related to poorer treatment outcomes, such as: lack of symptom stabilization, homelessness, lower quality of life and hospitalization.

Purpose: This chapter aims to discuss adherence to treatment to social anxiety disorder and possible interventions to increase adherence.

Results: It was found that some patients on a social phobia research had a poor adherence to group psychotherapy, some of them having abandoned therapy at different stages. The results showed that those patients had a history of poor adherence to other treatments, a misunderstanding of their treatment outcomes and clinical status, lack of motivation and attribution of their symptoms to personality features instead of the disease. Yet, a correlation between depression and active treatment was found (SSRI, CBT or combined). The patients with dependent personality trait adhered less to treatment. The antisocial and borderline disorders were correlated with low adherence in CBT. The presence or absence of social abilities before treatment was not related to adherence, different from what we found in the literature. Besides, social phobic patients adherence to treatment is likely to increase when family members also participate in the intervention.

Conclusion: Therapists should be concerned to patient's motivation and with his/her continuous evaluation of adherence in order to detect those who most likely would abandon the treatment in order to prevent patients, initially motivated, discouraged with the treatment and consequently leaving. The findings of personality disorders indicate the need to deal with these disorders before or concomitant the treatment of social phobia. A possible solution to increase adherence to mental disorders patients, particularly anxiety illnesses, is to consider the family as an active and central figure in the patient's treatment. Therefore, adherence interventions that include family as an important variable are likely to succeed.

Chapter 4 – Because acute pain is unpleasant sensory associated with fear and worries it is common reason that somebody seek a medical help. In some cases, even after it has been appropriate treated, it may persist and develop from acute into chronic form. In this article the authors pay attention to this, to the traditional biomedical treatment generally difficult accessible pain, which significant worse the individual's quality of life. The adherence to treatment, usually combination of pharmacological and physical therapies, they highlighted through individual's changed life position, ways of coping, as well as from the viewpoint of theoretical models, which could predict and explain health behaviour and adherence in medical treatment.

After a torment of diagnostic procedures and testing the effects of various available medical options, chronic pain patients could be completely frustrated and deep rooted in a passive, "sick role". Therefore primary goal in psychological treatment as a part of multidimensional, multidisciplinary, and multimodal approach to pain management must be shifting toward interventions emphasizing a proactive and self-management capacity of the patients. But this raises the questions of their motivation. The solutions can be seen in integrative therapeutic approach including the models of provider-patients interactions such as the Motivating Interviewing, MI, and Patient-Centred Model with the principles of Self management concept.

In: Adherence to Treatment in Clinical Practice   ISBN: 978-1-63117-841-2
Editor: Pamela Lofland   © 2014 Nova Science Publishers, Inc.

Chapter 1

CLINICAL TREATMENT OUTCOMES

Kathy Sexton-Radek
Elmhurst College, Elmhurst, IL, US
Suburban Pulmonary & Sleep Associates, Westmont, IL, US

ABSTRACT

The literature that examines adherence to treatment is represented in this chapter. Adherence to medical regimens and medication has been predominantly represented in this literature base. However, Behavioral interventions are described in terms of mental health treatments and psychoeducational approaches have also been included in this literature. The methodology predominantly, in a majority of the investigations, was survey based with random treatment control used for outcome measures of medication adherence. Treatment adherence is commonly referenced to these medication adherence studies. Some conclusions are presented for the reader. It is concluded from the findings in this area, that mild levels of adherence to treatment exists.

Keywords: Adherence, treatment compliance, clinical treatment adherence

The issue to identify and minimize patient behaviors that lead to their non-adoption of clinician recommended treatments is complicated. Estimates vary from 15 to 93% of non-adherence (DiMatteo, 2004). Researchers estimate the average of 26% non-adherence across all treatments (DiMatteo, 2004). Some

80% of patients fail to adhere to behavioral changes such as smoking cessation. It has been reported that adherence is highest for HIV, arthritis, gastrointestinal disorders and cancer and lowest among patient with pulmonary disease, diabetes and sleep disorders (DiMatteo, 2004). The Center for Advancement of Health has focused research on the adherence topic; it has the following recommendations: 1) Make adult literacy a natural priority; 2) Require all prescriptions to be types on a keyboard; 3) Make an electronic record; 4) Enforce requirements that pharmacists provide clear instructions and counseling along with prescription medications; 5) Develop checklists for both patients and doctors so they can ask and answer the right questions before a prescription is written (Center for Health, 2009). Turk and Meichenbaum (1991) reported adherences highest when the advice is "medical" (90%), when "vocational (70%), and psychological or social is the lowest rate (60%).

INTRODUCTORY ISSUES

Some patients engage in creative non-adherence such as adapting the medication to a fewer days per week affordability. Cooper, Love and Raffoul (1982) reported non-adherence among the elderly was intentional 76% of the time rather than accidental. Patients also employ their understanding of their condition to their medical regime using schedules divergent from what was prescribed and substituting with over the counter medication. After time, the alterations also include days without medication or taking too much medication or any other variation on a medication regime schedule other than the medically-pharmacologically.

A majority of literature on adherence addresses the provider-patient relationship. Improvement of provider communication receives the major focus in the literature. DiMatteo (2004) provided specific suggestions, those are provided appendix A. Kabat-Zinn and Chapman (1988) reported the need to ask the patient what they intend to do as it will assist the provider in understanding their barriers to treatment adherence.

Additional measures are needed to address social/psychological non-adherence rates. The Information Motivation-Behavior Skills Model of Health Behavior reinforces the need for motivation to adhere, skills to perform the behavior and the right information for treatment adherence. Figure 1 depicts this relationship. The provider's role is significant within the application if this model is used and a physician provider encourages the use of a program (Kabat-Zinn & Chapmen-Waldrop, 1988). Medical problems that present with psychological symptoms are represented in Table 1. Several topics have been identified as important to pursue in an effort to address adherence to treatment in Appendix A.

Mental health treatments are creatively varied. Lyons, Howard, O'Mahoney and Lisk (1997) proposed a classification of mental health services as case management, day treatment, psychosocial and vocational rehabilitation, drop-in sessions, community outreach/prevention. Patients with severe and persistent psychiatric disorders utilize community-based services with measurable levels of outcome, usually after six months (Lyons, et al., 1997). McNicholas (2012) writes of the importance patient adherence to treatment as predictive of outcome (along with treatment effectiveness). Methodical difficulties in studies, definition and measurement problems have been identified as problem areas in treatment adherence investigations (McNicholas, 2012).

Table 1. Medical Problems that Present with Psychological Symptoms

Hypothyroidism:	Lethargy, anxiety, irritability, thought disorder, somatic delirium, hallucination, paranoia
Systematic Lupus Erythematosus:	Varied presentation, thought disorder, depression. confusion
Vitamin B Deficiencies:	Clinical evidence of vitamin deficiency occurs only when tissue stores are sharply depleted and these include sore tongue, weakness, paresthesias, lemon yellow complexion, visual disturbances
Pernicious anemia:	Depression, guilt feelings, confusion, weight loss

Source: R. C. Hall (Ed.). (1980). Psychiatric presentation of medical illness: Somatopsychic disorders. New York: SP Medical and Scientific Books.

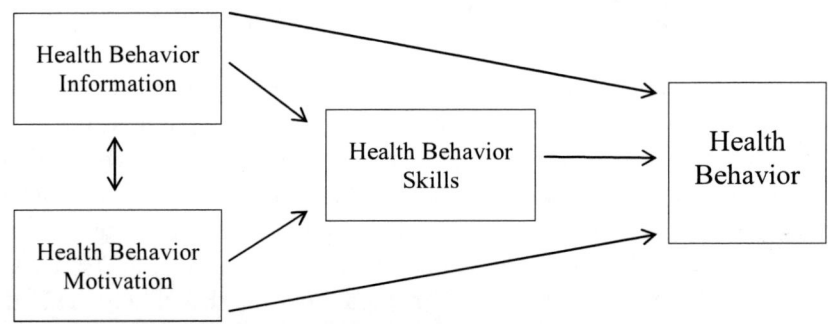

Source: Fisher, Fisher, Amico, & Harmon, 2006.

Figure 1. Information Motivation-Behavioral Skills Model of Health Behavior.

Table 2. Topics Explored for Research and Treatment Adherence

good communication have them repeat women & caring	perceive provider ignoring behavior answer their questions ask pt. decision to adhere
lack of time no money	OTC / Home remedies instability
Adherence Ratings Scales Research methods – Applied	Self-Efficacy

The World Health Organization defines adherence as "the degree to which the personal behaviors, taking medication, following a diet and or executing lifestyle changes corresponds with the agreed recommendation of a health care provider." The costs of non-adherence are estimated to be approximately $300 billion a year in the United States. These costs resulted from increased hospital visit, unnecessary hospitalizations and increased disease expression/mortality and morbidity Haynes, Taylor and Sackett (1979).

In the field of mental health, adherence studies have focused on medication adherence with little attention to behavioral interventions. Outcome variables such as quality of life, improved relationships and self-report are less commonly used (Neil, Batterhron, Christensen, Bennet and Griffiths, 2009). Another methodological limitation is in terms of the timing of the measurement. This critique has occurred in that the predominant measurement of medication adherence does not take into account confounding (e.g., family, social, environmental factors that influence a patient's readiness to take medication), measures and illness/disease course (Haynes, Montage, Oliver, McKibbon, Brouwers & Kanari, 2001; Meichenbaum & Turk, 1987).

RESEARCH METHODS EMPLOYED

Suggestions in the literature to ameliorate the methodological issues are to more closely examining traditional methods of medication adherence in terms of patterns of days missed, timings of taking medications. Toward this end adherence measurements using technological advances of counting medication taking when the cap is removed from the pill bottle are sometimes used (Henriques, Costa, and Cabrita, 2012). The methods used in this study were exemplary with a random control method and the Cochrone method of evaluation of risk bias – that is, a two-step method to examine domains of sequence generation, allocation concealment, incomplete outcome data, selective outcome reporting and other potential threats to validity. Hill, et al.

(2011) provided an analysis of five studies that appears in Table 2. The studies relied on self-report to determine adherence, with other components of the study denoting strong methodological quality and low risk of bias (Hill and Kavookjian, 2011).

More specific approaches to the examination of adherence are conducted by population (Berkowitz, Bell, Kravitz and Feldman, 2012; Billinek and Sorkin, 2011; Charach, Figueroa, Chen, Ickowicz and Schachar, 2006; Devatharshy, Charach and Schachar, 2001; Fotheringham, 1993; Ngo-Metzer, Sorkin, Billinek, Greenfield & Kaplan, 2011; Simon and Duncan, 2012; Wheeler, Wagamon, McCord, 2012) and provider/setting variables (Evers, Klusman, Schwarzor and Heuser, 2012; Gaffney, Kitsantas and Cheema, 2011;Hall, Roter, and Katz, 1988; Haynes, Ackloo, Sahota, McDonald and Yao, 2008; Holt, Thorogood, and Grittiths, 2011; Norman, Conner, and Bell, 2000; Piette et al., 2005; Stalmeier, 2011; Woldu et al., 2011).

Patient's Perspectives

Rates of non-adherence are lower in non-developing countries. Some theorists have pointed out that western medicine is associated with authority and power that are perceived to threaten the patient's freedom. Behavioral treatments that require lifestyle changes for health and chronic illness behaviors are estimated to be about 50%. An example of such treatments, entail surveys of Adolescent patient compliance with their diabetes mellitus medication regimes; this survey is represented in Table 3 (Wheeler, Wagaman & McCord, 2012). A small number of behavioral studies of non-adherence have been focused on ADHD treatments with a 61% adherence reporting. A strong point of this area is that these studies have been rigorous randomized control treatment outcome studies. Mexican-Americans reported financial burdens due to their medical care as compared with other patients.

Patients' understanding of the treatment regime asked of them has received some study in the literature. Some examples from Health Psychology interventions focus on bolstering physician-patient communication by use of motivation interviewing and communication skills training (Axelsson, Cliffordson, Lundgre, and Brink, 2013; DiMatteo, Haskord and Williams, 2007; Gearing, Schwalbe and Short, 2012). Also, patients must understand the specifics of the treatment regime in terms of what is asked of them (Henriques, Costa and Cabrita, 2012; Zolnierek and DiMatteo, 2009). Some treatment outcome studies have noted patients' prognosis, level of insight into their illness, previous treatment, number/extent of relapse and level of patients' understanding of procedures. With this are elements of patient's education level, trust/belief in the effectiveness of the intervention (Axelsson, Cliffordson, Lundgren and Brink, 2012; Gearing, Schwalbe and Short, 2012).

Evers and Klusman (2012) identified physical activity programs to be of lowered adherence as compared to mental health programs. The use of coping plans on number of coping plan formation was reported to mediate the relationship between intention and behavior. Coping plans are a type of Health Behavior Skills that can be trained in patients once the information and motivation to achieve a healthy behavior are evident; this relationship is depicted in Figure 1 (Fisher, Fisher, Amico & Harmon, 2006).

Shippe et al. (2012) reported adherence variations of colorectal cancer screen (79%), mammography (89%), cervical cancer screen (91%), tetanus immunizations (82%) and pneumococcal vaccination (62%). Stalmeier (2011) indicated the need to determine decision pathways and develop corresponding decision aid to assist patients. The technical quality of the materials such as appearance, reading level and message are paramount to patient understanding. Motivational interviewing has been implemented in Physician training programs as a means of increasing the quality of communication and adherence with the patient. An example of the utility of motivational interviewing with highly active antiretroviral therapies (HAART) used with HIV patients.

Simon and Damian (2012) reported estimates of 36-83% non-adherence for CPAP use (i.e., fewer than four hours use per night). The rates for youth CPAP adherence were estimated to be lower than this. Simon and Damian (2012) reported the utility of open communication with all family members to determine the health perception.

Axelsson (2013) identified the personality factor of self-efficacy as influenced in mediating health related behaviors adherence. These findings were determined from a sample with chronic illness. Roecklein and Schumacher (2012) suggested the use of support and self-efficacy when examining adherence variables of bright light therapy in the treatment of seasonal affective disorder. The person variables of support and estimation of the belief that a patient has of following through with a medical treatment are substantive.

Table 3. Overview of Studies

Source	Study design	Sample	Intervention duration, type, and group details	Adherence measuring instrument	Adherence results and outcomes	Clinical outcomes measured	Clinical general results	Details
Pradier et al. (France, 2003)	Randomized controlled trial	202 HIV positive patients	Six months (three session); in person C: Medical consultation every 2-3 months I: Offered program with three MI sessions	Self-reported	Case>Control; adherence at 6-month follow-up: I: 75% C: 61% (p=0.04)	Viral load	Significant difference in mean difference of viral load between baseline and 6-month follow-up for intervention group	Mean difference in intervention group: -0.22log, mean difference in the control group: +.22log, (p=0.013 for intervention group, p=0.014 for control group)
Golin et al. (USA, 2006)	Randomized controlled trial	141 HIV positive patients	Two months (Two visits); in person, audiotape, workbook, and mailed booster C: Educational audiotape and workbook with two educational sessions I: Behavioral audiotape and workbook with two MI sessions	Composite Adherence Score (CAS): pill counts, self-reporting, and eDEMS cap	Case = Control; adherence after 2 months: I: 76% C: 71% (p=0.62)	Coping, change in viral load	No significant difference in coping or change in viral load	n/a for viral load, p=0.0629 for coping

Table 3. (Continued)

Source	Study design	Sample	Intervention duration, type, and group details	Adherence measuring instrument	Adherence results and outcomes	Clinical outcomes measured	Clinical general results	Details
Samet et al. (USA, 2003)	Randomized controlled trial	151 HIV positive patients with a history of alcohol problems	Three months (three visits); in person C: Standard care for HIV patient I: MI sessions with one follow-up home visit	Self-reported	Case = Control; no significant differences in adherence reported ($p>0.25$)	CD4 count, viral load, alcohol consumption	No significant differences in any secondary outcomes	All p values >0.25
Parsons et al. (USA, 2007)	Randomized controlled trial	143 HIV positive hazardous drinking patients	Three months (eight visits); in person C: eight session educational program I: eight session MI interventions	Self-reported	Case > Control; patients receiving intervention reported a significantly larger increase in percent dose and percent day adherence than control counterparts (p,0.05 for percent dose adherence, p,0.05 for percent day adherence)	Viral load, CD4, drinking behavior	Significant decrease in viral load and increase in CD4 count at 3 months, not sustained at 6 months. No significant difference in drinking behavior	IC decreased viral load at 3-month follow-up and control group increase viral load, but did not sustain difference at 6-month follow-up. IC achieved significantly higher CD4 count than CG, but statistical significance was not reached at 6-month follow-up. (p,0.02 for viral load at 3 months)

Source	Study design	Sample	Intervention duration, type, and group details	Adherence measuring instrument	Adherence results and outcomes	Clinical outcomes measured	Clinical general results	Details
DiIorio et al. (USA, 2008)	Randomized controlled trial	326 HIV positive patients	Three months (five sessions) with a 10-month follow-up period; in person and over phone C: normal care for HIV patient I: Individual MI counseling sessions	MEMS cap	Case > Control; Intervention group participants took significantly greater percentage of doses on time compared to control group counterparts. ($p=0.05$)	CD4 count and viral load	No significant differences in any secondary outcomes	Participants achieving undetectable viral load at 6-month follow-up: **I**: 58 **C**: 47 ($p=0.410$); mean CD4 count at follow: **I**: 227 **C**: 262 ($p=0.937$)

Note: C, Control; I, Intervention.
Source: Hill & Kavookjian (2012).

ASSESSMENT METHODS

The Treatment Adherence Questionnaire for Patients with Hypertension has psychometric ratings (Cronbach alphas of 0.88, 0.82 for test-retest reliability). Self-report measures, interviews and diary methods have been recommended for the measurement of adherence (DiMatteo, 2004). The Medication Adherence Scale, Hill-Borne Compliance to High Blood Pressure Therapy Scale and Medication Adherence Self-Efficacy Scale has been reported to be adequate in the measurement of medication adherence (Ma, Chen, You, Luo and Xing, 2011).

Of equal value in such studies is the use of patient literacy level scales and complete histories to including factors that may confound search for health such as obesity. The Rapid Estimate of Adult Literacy in Medicine provides a quick measure of patient health literacy (Shaw and Bosworth, 2011).

Significant relationships have been found with samples of schizophrenia diagnosed patients treated with psychotropic medications for three months or greater, side effects, and increasing values of non-adherence. An investigation measuring adherence to depression medication reported the importance of vicarious experience (i.e., knowing a friend or family member with depression) to be predictive of greater adherence (DiBonaventure, Gabriel, Dupclay, Gupta and Kim, 2012; Morisky, Ang and Krousel, 2008).

In groups of elderly patients, the relationship with nurses has been identified as influential in their adherence to medication regimes (Henriques et al., 2012). The explanation of inserting the medication taking into their daily life has been emphasized as an enhancing factor to the patient-nurse relationship. Relationships with care providers to increase adherence has also been employed in the area of parent training to assist in their care of infant feeding behaviors. An outcome variable of weight for age increased when intervention behaviors of no bottle to bed, minimal juice consumption, breast feeding throughout first year of life and introduction to solid food no earlier than 46 months was adhered to by parents (Gaffney, Kitsantas and Cheema, 2011).

Personality factors of conscientiousness, agreeableness and extraversion personality domains was related to self-reported adherence with a regime for diabetes management for adolescents. Table 4 lists the Adolescent Adherence questionnaire that, along with the NEO-PI-R was taken by adolescents diagnosed with diabetes mellitus type 1 and assigned to medication and diet intervention (Wheeler, 2012). Gearing, Schwalbe and Short (2012) identified promoters of adolescent adherence to psychosocial treatment as therapeutic and barriers to adherence in the family domain were described as parent understanding of the adolescent patient's condition and need to participate in the psychosocial program. Adolescent barriers to adherence in attendance and investment in the psychosocial intervention program (Gearing et al., 2012).

Table 4. Adolescent Questionnaire

1. How often do you check your blood sugar in a day? • Sporadic or no monitoring of my blood sugar (score = 0) • 1 time per day, 3 or more times a week (score = 1) • 2 times per day, 3 or more times a week (score = 2) • 3 or more times per day, 3 or more times a week (score = 3)
2. Which method best describes the manner in which you take your insulin? • Skips insulin doses or forgets often; refuses a 2nd shot when it is needed (score = 0) • Changes dosage amount (i.e., following sliding scale) only with advice by another person; occasionally misses or administers insulin very late (i.e., after the appropriate or designated time when the insulin was supposed to be administered, such as after a meal rather than before a meal). (score = 1) • Technique and timing of insulin administration is good; injection site rotation is good; insulin is always taken and almost always at the appropriate or designed time; occasionally adjusts insulin dose when necessary (based on blood sugar levels, exercise, or diet). (score =2) • Technique and timing of insulin administration is excellent; injection site rotation is excellent; insulin is always taken and always at the appropriate or designed time; always adjusts insulin dose appropriately as indicated by blood glucose level, exercise and diet. (score = 3)
3. How well do you adhere to the diabetic diet prescribed by your doctor? • I make little or no effort to follow my diabetic diet; I never count carbohydrates/food exchanges or rarely carbohydrates/food exchanges. (score=0) • Amount of food eaten and time at which food is eaten inconsistent 50% of the time; I occasionally forget or refuse to count carbohydrates/food exchanges. (score=1) • Amount of food eaten and time at which food is eaten is consistent 50-90% of the time; I almost always count carbohydrates/food exchanges. (score=2)
• Amount of food eaten and time at which food is eaten is consistent 90-100% of the time; I have adjusted very well to my prescribed diet (score=3)
4. How frequently do you exercise or engage in a physical activity or sport during the week? • times a week (score=0) • 1-2 time a week (score=1) • 3-4 times a week (score=2) • 5 or more times a week (score=3)

Table 4. (Continued)

5. How would you rate your overall knowledge about diabetes (including diabetic complications, symptoms of high and low blood sugar reactions, proper methods for checking blood sugar and administering insulin, diet, exercise, and other information you know about diabetes? • Poor • Fair • Good • Excellent
6. Have you ever attended educational sessions about diabetes?   Yes   No If yes, what kind? _____ Where were these sessions held? Hospital Outpatient setting Doctor office Camp School Other__ How many times did you attend the educational sessions? Check which types of topics were discussed in the educational sessions: • Proper timing/method to check blood sugar • Proper time/method to administer insulin • How to determine the amount of insulin that should be administered • Symptoms of high/low blood sugar reactions and diabetic complication • Diet and nutrition (what to eat, when to eat, how to count carbs/food exchanges, how and who food affects blood sugar, etc.)
7. Who takes *primary* responsibility in monitoring/managing your diabetes? • Mother (or female guardian) • Father (or male guardian) • Self • Other
8. What was the result/level of your last hemoglobin (HbA1c) test?_____

Source: Wheeler, Wagaman, & McCord, 2012.

CONCLUSION

Mild clinical treatment adherence exists. Studies have found medication primarily although behavioral treatment adherence has had some support. Both specific and general measures of assessment have been utilized. Future directions indicate the need more uniform investment in the measurement of treatment adherence.

APPENDIX A.

1. Listen to patient.
2. Ask patient to repeat about how to be done.
3. Keep the prescription as simple as possible.
4. Give clear instructions on the exact treatment regime, preferable in writing.
5. Make use of special reminder pill containers and calendars.
6. Call the patent if an appointment is missed.
7. Prescribe a self-care regime in concert with the patient's daily schedule.
8. Explain at each visit the important of adherence.
9. Gear the frequency of visits to adherence needs.
10. Acknowledge at each visit the patient's efforts to adhere.
11. Involve the patient's spouse or other partner.
12. Whenever possible provide the patient with instructions and advice at the start of the information to be presented.
13. When providing the patient with instructions and advice, stress how important they are.
14. Use short words and short sentences.
15. Use explicit categorization where possible. (for example, divide information clearly into categories of etiology, treatment, or prognosis.)
16. Repeat things, when feasible.
17. When giving advice, make it as specific, detailed and concrete as possible.
18. Find out what the patient's worries are. Do no confine yourself merely to gathering objective medical information.
19. Find out what the patient's expectations are. If they cannot be met, explain why.
20. Provide information about the diagnosis and the cause of the illness.
21. Adopt a friendly rather than a business-like attitude.
22. Avoid medical jargon.
23. spend some time in conversation about non-medical topics.
24. have them repeat their question, gently repeat your response/ information
25. answer their questions
26. ask about their lack of time to do the task

27. ask about the extent of OTC / Home remedies
28. ask if there is money/financial instability that is blocking their following through with treatment

Source: DiMatteo, 2004.

REFERENCES

American Public Health Association. (2004). Adherence to HIV treatment regimens: recommendations for best practices APHA.

Armbruster, P. & Kazdin, A. E. (1994). Attrition in child psychotherapy. *Advances in Clinical Child Psychology, 16*, 81-109.

Avins, A., Pressman, A., Ackerson, L., Rudd, P., Neuhaus, J. & Vittinghoff, E. (2010). Placebo adherence and its association with morbidity and mortality in the studies of left ventricular dysfunction. *J Gen Intern Med, 25*(12), 1275-1281.

Avius, A., Pressmen, A., Ackerman, L., Rudd, P., Newhause, J. & Vittinghoff, E. (2010). Placebo adherence and its association with morbidity and mortality in the studies of left ventricular dysfunction. *Journal of General Internal Medicine, 25*(12), 1275-1281.

Axelsson, M., Cliffordson, C., Lundgren, J. & Brink, E. (2013). Self-efficacy and adherence as mediating factors between personality traits and health-related quality of life. *Quality Life Research, 22*, 567-575.

Berkowitz, S. A., Bell, R. A., Kravitz, R. L. & Feldman, M. D. (2012). Vicarious experience affects patients' treatment preferences for depression. *PLos ONE, 7*(2), e 31269.

Billinek, J. & Sorkin, D. (2011). Self-reported neighborhood safety and non-adherence to treatment regimens among patients with Type 2 Diabetes. *Journal of General Internal Medicine, 27*(3), 292-296.

Bussing, R. & Koro-Ljungberg, M. E., Gary. (2005) Exploring help seeking for ADHD symptoms; a mixed methods approach. *Har Rev Psychiatry, 13*, 85-101.

Center for the Advancement of Health. (2009). Taking charge of your health records. *The Prepared Patient, 2*, 1-2.

Charach, A., Figueroa, M., Chen, S., Ickowicz, A. & Schachar, R. (2006). Stimulant treatment over 5 years: effects on growth. *Am Acad Child Adolesc Psychiatry., 45*(4), 415-21.

Cooper, J. K., Love, D. W. & Rafford, P. R. (1982). Intentional prescription non-adherence (non-compliance) by the elderly. *Journal of the American Geriatric Society, 38*, 329-333.

Demyttenaere, K. (1998). Noncompliance with antidepressants: who's to blame? *Int Clin Psychopharmacol, 13*(Suppl 2), S19-S25.

Devatharshy, T., Charach, A. & Schachar, R. (2001). Moderators and mediators of long-term adherence to stimulant treatment in children with ADHD. *J Acad Child Adolesc Psychiatry, 40*(8), 922-928.

DiBonaventure, M., Gabriel, S., Dupclay, C., Gupta, S. & Kim, E. (2012). A patient perspective of the impact of medication side effects on adherence: Results of cross-sectional nationwide survey of patients with schizophrenia. *Biomedical Central Psychiatry, 12*, 20.

DiMatteo, M. R. (2004). Social support and patient adherence to medical treatment: a meta-analysis. *Health Psychology, 23,* 207-218.

DiMatteo, M. R., Haskord, K. B. & Williams, S. L. (2007). Health beliefs, disease severity and patient adherence: A meta-analysis. *Medical Care, 47*(8), 521-528.

Evers, A., Klusmann, V., Schwarzor, R. & Heuser, I. (2012). Adherence to physical and mental activity interventions: Coping plans as a mediator and prior adherence as a moderator. *British Journal of Psychology, 17*, 477-491.

Fishbein, M., Triandis, H. & Kanfer, F. (2001). *Factors influencing behaviour and behaviour change*. In: Baum A, Revenson T, Sing J (eds) Handbook of health psychology. Erlbaum, Mahway

Fisher, J. D., Fisher W. A., Amico, K. R. & Harmon, J. J. (2006). An information motivation behavior and skills model of adherence to anti-retroviral therapy. *Health Psychology, 25*, 462-473.

Fotheringham, M. S. (1993). Adherence to recommended medical regimens in childhood and adolescence. *Journal Pediatric Child Health, 31*, 72-78.

Gaffney, K. F., Kitsantas, P. & Cheema, J. (2011). Clinical practice guidelines for feeding behaviors and weight-for-age at 12 months: A secondary analysis of the infant feeding practices study II. *Worldviews on Evidence Based Nursing*, 234-242.

Gearing, R. E., Schwalbe, C. S. & Short, K. D. (2012). Adolescent adherence to psychosocial treatment: Mental health clinician's perspectives on barriers and promoters. *Psychotherapy Research, 22*(3), 317-321.

Hall, J. A., Roter, D. L. & Katz, N. R. (1988). Meta-analysis of correlates of provider behaviour in medical encounters. *Med Care, 26*, 657-675.

Haynes, R. B., Montage, P., Oliver, T., McKibbon, K. A., Brouwers, M. C. & Kanari, R. (2001). *Interventions for helping patients follow prescriptions for medications.* Cochrane Libr. (Oxford) 1 (28p) (19 ref 23 bib).

Haynes, R. B., Taylor, D. W. & Sackett, D. L. (1979). *Compliance in health care.* Baltimore, MD: Johns Hopkins University Press.

Haynes, R. B., Ackloo, E., Sahota, N., McDonald, H. P. & Yao, X. (2008). Interventions for enhancing medication adherence Cochrane Database Syst Rev Issue 2. Art No: CD0000011.doi:10.1002/14651858.CD0000011.pub3.

Henriques, M. A., Costa, M. A. & Cabrita, J. (2012). Adherence and medication management by the elderly. *Journal of Clinical Nursing, 21*, 3096-3105.

Hill, S. & Kavookjian, J. (2012). Motivational interviewing as a behavioral intervention to increase HAART adherence in patients who are HIV positive: A systematic review of the literature. *AIDS Care, 25(5)*, 583-592.

Holt, T. A., Thorogood, M. & Grittiths, F. (2011). Changing clinical practice through patient specific reminders available at the time of the clinical encounter: Systematic review and meta-analysis. *Journal of General Internal Medicine, 27*(8), 974-984.

Kabat-Zinn, J. & Chapman-Waldrop, A. (1988). Compliance with an outpatient stress reduction program: Rates and predictors of program completion. *Journal of Behavioral Medicine, 11*, 333-352.

Lyons, J. S. & Weiner, D. A., (Eds.). *Strategies in Behavioral Healthcare: Total Clinical Outcomes Management.* New York City, New York, Civic Research Institute, 2008.

Ma, C., Chen, S., You, L., Luo, Z. & Xiing, C. (2011). Development and psychometric evaluation of the Treatment Adherence Questionnaire for patients with hypertension. *Journal of Advanced Nursing, 68*(6), 1402-1413.

Marcus, S. C. & Durkin, M. (2011) Stimulant adherence and academic performance in urban youth with attention-deficit/hyperactivity disorder. *J Am Acad Child Adolesc Psychiarry, 50*(5), 480-489.

McNicholas, F. (2012). To adhere or not and what we can do to help. *European Child Adolescent Psychiatry, 21*, 657-663.

Meichenbaum, D. & Turk, D. C. (1987). *Facilitating treatment adherence: A practitioner's guidebook.* New York: Plenum.

Morisky, D. E., Ang, A. & Krousel, W. M. (2008). Predictive validity of a medication adherence measure in an outpatient setting. *Journal of Clinical Hypertension, 10*(5), 348-354.

Neil, A. L., Batterhron, P., Christensen, H., Bennet, K. & Griffiths, K. M. (2009). Predictors of adherence to adolescents to a cognitive behavior therapy website in school and community-based settings. *Journal Medical Internal Research, 11(1),* 6.

Ngo-Metzger, Q., Sorkin, D. H., Billinek, J., Greenfield, S. & Kaplan, S. H. (2011). The effects of financial pressure on adherence and glucose control among racial/ethnically diverse patients with diabetes. *Journal of General Internal Medicine, 27*(4), 432-437.

Pappadopulos, E., Jensen, P. S., Chait, A. R., Arnold, L. E., Swanson, J. M., Greenhill, L. L., Hecthman, L., Chuang, S., Wells, K. C., Pelham, W., Cooper, T., Elliott, G. & Newcom, J. H. (2009). Medication adherence in the MTA: saliva methylphenidate samples versus parent report and mediating effect of concomitant behavioral treatment. *J Am. Acad Child Adolesc Psychiatry, 48*(5), 501-510.

Pekarik, G. & Finney-Owen, K. (1987). Outpatient clinic therapist attitudes and beliefs relevant to client dropout. *Community Mental Health Journal, 23*(2), 120-130.

Peveler, R., George, C., Kinmonth, A. & Campbell, M. Thompson. (1999). Effect of antidepressant drug counselling and information leaflets on adherence to drug treatment in primary care: randomised controlled trial. *Br Med J, 319,* 612-615.

Piette, J. D. et al. (2005). The role of patient-physician trust in moderating medication non-adherence due to cost pressure. *Archive Internal Medicine, 165*(15), 1749-1755.

Roecklein, K. A., Schumacher, J. A., Miller, M. A. & Ernecoff, N.C. (2012). Cognitive and behavior predictors of light therapy use. *PLosONE, 7(6),* e 39275.

Sabaté. E. (2001) WHO Adherence Meeting Report. Geneva World Health Organization, Adherence to long term therapies, Policy for Action. http://www.who.int/chp/knowledge/ublications/adherencerep.pdf.

Shaw, R. & Bosworth, H. B. (2011). Baseline medication adherence and blood pressure in a 24-monthlongitudenal hypertension study. *Journal of Clinical Nursing, 21,* 1401-1406.

Shea, S., DuMouchel, W. & Bahamonde, L. (1996). A meta-analysis of 16 randomized control trial to evaluate computer-based clinical reminder systems for preventive care in the ambulatory setting. *Journal of American Medical Information Association, 3*(6), 399-409.

Shipee, N. D., Mullan, R. J., Nabhau, M. Kermott, C. A., Hagen, P. T., Rhodes, D. J., Montori, V. M. & Murad, M. H. (2012). Adherence to preventive recommendations: Experience of a cohort presenting for executive health care. *Population Health Management, 15*(2), 65-71.

Simon, S. L. & Duncan, C. L. (2012). Objective and subjective health parameters and relation to CPAP adherence in pediatric obstructive sleep apnea. *Children's Health Care, 41*, 223-232.

Stalmeier, P. F. (2011). Adherence and decision aids: A model and narrative review. *Medical Decision Making, 31*, 121-129.

Taylor, S. E., Repetti, R. L. & Seeman, T. (1997). Health psychology: What is an unhealthy environment and how does it get under the skin? *Annual Review of Psychology, 48*(1), 411-447.

Turk, D. C. & Meichenbaum, D. (1991). Adherence to self-care regimes. In J.J. Sweet, R.H. Rozensky & S.M. Tovian (Eds.). *Handbook of clinical psychology in medical settings* (249-266). New York: Plenum.

Vermeire, E. I. J. J., Wens, J., Van Royen, P., Biot, Y., Hearnshaw, H. & Lindenmeyer, A. (2005). Interventions for improving adherence to treatment recommendations in people with type 2 diabetes mellitus. *Cochrane Database Syst Rev Issue 2*. Art. No.: CD003638. doi: 10.1002/14651858.CD3638.pub2

Weis, S. E., Slocum, P. C., Blais, F. X., King, B., Nunn, M. G., Matney, B., Gomez, E. & Foresman, B. H. (1994). The effect of directly observed therapy on the rates of drug resistance and relapse in tuberculosis. *N Engl J Med, 330*, 1179-1184.

Wheeler, K., Wagamon, A. & McCord, D. (2012). Personality traits as predictors of adherence in adolescents with Type 1 Diabetes. *Journal of Child and Adolescent Psychiatric Nursing, 25*, 68-74.

Wierzybiki, M. & Pekarik, G. (1993). A meta-analysis of psychotherapy dropout. *Profession Psychology: Research and Practice, 24*, 190-195.

Woldu, H., Goldstein, T., Sakolsky, D., Perel, J., Emslie, G., Mayes, T., Clarke, G., Ryan, N. D., Birmaher, B., Wagner, K. D., Asarnow, J. R., Keller, M. B. & Brent, D. (2011) Pharmacokinetically and clinician-determined adherence to an antidepressant regimen and clinical outcome in the TORIDA trial. *J Am Acad Child Adolesc Psychiatry, 50*(5), 490-498

World Health Organisation, (2003) *Adherence to long term therapies, evidence for action.* http://whqlibdoc.who.int/publications/2003/9241545992.pdf.

Zolnierek, K. B. & DiMatteo, M. R. (2009). Physician communication and patient adherence to treatment: A meta-analysis. *Medical Care, 47(8)*, 826-839.

In: Adherence to Treatment in Clinical Practice
Editor: Pamela Lofland

ISBN: 978-1-63117-841-2
© 2014 Nova Science Publishers, Inc.

Chapter 2

THEORETICAL MODELS OF ADHERENCE

Sara Garfield[1,2]

[1]The Centre for Medication Safety and Service Quality, Imperial College Healthcare NHS Trust, London, UK
[2]UCL, School of Pharmacy, London, UK

ABSTRACT

In this chapter theoretical models of adherence to medical treatment are reviewed. The chapter begins by describing the traditional biomedical approach and then moves on to explain the broader psychological approaches including: the health belief model, health locus of control theory, self efficacy theory, the theory of planned behaviour, the self-regulatory model and the transtheroetical stages of change model. The limitations of these psychological models are discussed and a more contemporary view of adherence using the accident causation framework is described. Finally, a move away from only focussing on adherence to incorporating other concepts such as shared decision making is described. For each model, the effects of the theoretical approach on the types of interventions that are employed to monitor and reduce non –adherence to treatment are discussed.

Keywords: Adherence, theoretical models, concordance, shared-decision making

THE BIOMEDICAL MODEL

Traditionally, medical adherence has been viewed as the extent to which a patient follows a prescriber's instructions. In this model, the assumption is that of a paternalistic relationship between the prescriber and patient. The terminology used is compliance rather than adherence, which implies it is the patients' responsibility to follow instructions given and that they are at fault if they do not do this. From this perspective, interventions to improve compliance are limited to educating patients so that they are better willing and able to comply with instructions.

EXPLANATORY PSYCHOLOGICAL MODELS

Psychological models approach adherence from the perspective of understanding patients' medication taking behaviour as a function of different constructs related to their health beliefs and experiences. When working within these models, interventions aiming to increase adherence are based on trying to influence these constructs in order to facilitate changes to healthcare behaviour. There are a vast number of models, which differ in the constructs included and the underlying theory. Some of the more commonly used models include the health belief model (Rosenstock 1974, Becker 1994), health locus of control theory (Wallston et al., 1978), self efficacy theory (Bandura 1977), the theory of planned behaviour (Ajzen 1991), the self regulatory model (Leventhal 1992) and the trantheroetical stages of change model (Proschaska, & Diclemente 1992).

The Health Belief Model (Rosenstock 1974, Becker 1994)

The health belief model (Rosenstock 1974, Becker 1994) views adherence as the result of the perceived threat of an illness, a cost-benefit analysis of taking action, cues to action and enabling and modifying factors (see Figure 1).

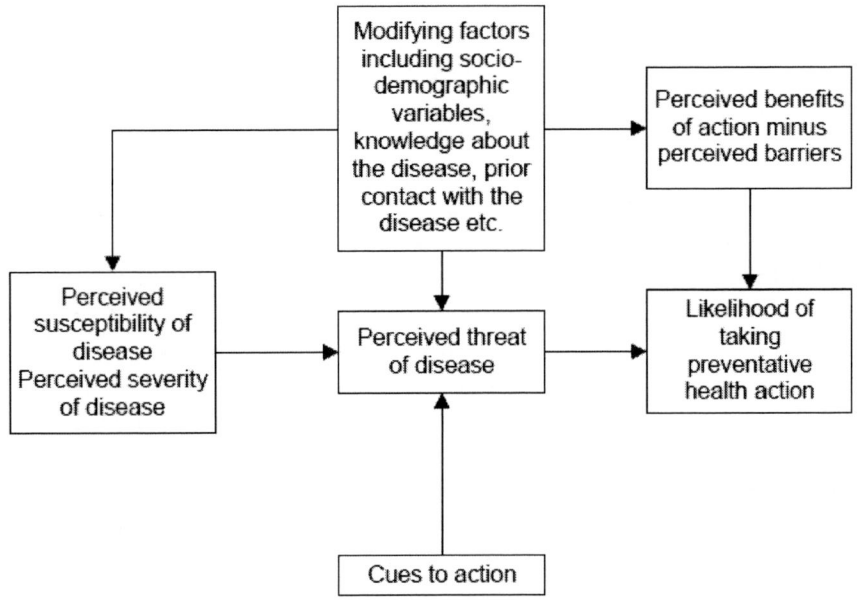

Figure 1. Health Belief Model.

The perceived threat consists of the perceived severity of an illness and the perceived susceptibility to it. If an illness is thought to be both serious and very likely to affect an individual they will be much more likely to decide to adhere to a regime designed to prevent or treat it. Individuals will also assess the perceived benefits of treatment with the perceived barriers to taking it. Examples of barriers are inconvenience and side effects of treatment. Cues to action are internal or external stimuli which motivate an individual towards adhering to treatment. These may include experiencing symptoms, illness in family and friends and health promotion campaigns. Finally modifying and enabling factors include age, gender, income and knowledge and experience with the disease.

From this more holistic perspective, interventions involving the heath belief model may include immediate cues to action such as healthcare publicity but could also act on reducing barriers such as minimising side effects by modifying regimes or inconvenience of treatment by finding ways to make it fit round patients' lives or making healthcare services themselves more flexible so that it becomes easier to access treatment.

The Health Locus of Control Theory (Wallston et al. 1978)

The health locus of control theory was developed using the principles of Rotter's (1996) learning theory. Rotter's (1996) theory was based on the principle that if an individual expects a particular reward for an action they are more likely to carry it out. Rotter (1996) divided individuals into two types; internals and externals. Internals are those who believe that outcomes occur as a result of an individual's own actions and are therefore under personal control. Externals believe that outcome are determined by factors beyond individual control. Wallston et al. (1978) applied this theory to health behaviour. He described individuals who believed their health was controlled by their own actions as having an internal locus of control. He divided external health locus of control into two categories, powerful others and chance. The model predicts that those individuals having an internal locus of control and those believing in healthcare professionals as powerful others will be more likely to be adherent to treatment. However, this will only be true for individuals who value health. Health locus of control may be used to predict the success of interventions to increase adherence.

The Self Efficacy Theory (Bandura 1977)

Social cognitive theory introduces the concept of self efficacy (Bandura 1977). Self efficacy is the product of efficacy expectations and outcome expectations. Efficacy expectations are the beliefs that an individual has regarding their ability to perform a behaviour and outcome expectations are the belief in the consequences of performing the behaviour. Efficacy expectations are derived from four sources: performance mastery (experiences of performing a task successfully), social modelling (seeing another person perform it successfully), social persuasion (encouragement from others) and psychological responses (the way an individual experiences a situation).

Interventions to increase adherence based on the self efficacy theory may focus on any of these four sources e.g., social persuasion in the form of health education and performance mastery in helping patients build skills needed to successfully carry out complex tasks such as exercise regimes or administering injections.

The Theory of Planned Behaviour (Ajzen 1991)

The theory of planned behaviour (Ajzen 1991) is based on the concept that an individual's behaviour will be associated with their intention. The intention will in turn be influenced by three factors: attitude to the behaviour, social norms (the perception of the way others view the behaviour) and perceived behavioural control (the extent to which an individual feels they have control over the behaviour- similar to self efficacy). According to this theory perceived behavioural control has a direct effect on behaviour as well as having an indirect effect through intention (see figure 2).

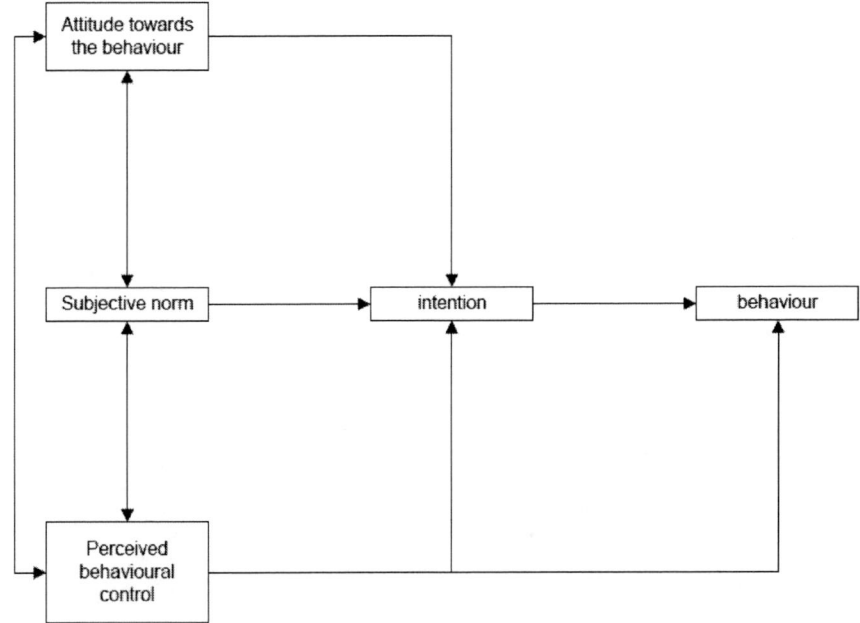

Azjen 1991.

Figure 2. Theory of Planned Behaviour Model.

From the perspective of the theory of planned behaviour, interventions may be based on trying to change attitudes to behaviour through education as well as through interventions designed to increase perceived behavioural control. The latter will be similar to those aimed at increasing self efficacy.

Self Regulatory Model (Leventhal 1992)

Leventhal's (1992) self regulatory model of adherence has three stages: interpretation of illness, development of coping strategies and appraisal of the coping strategies employed. At each of these three stages, two different components occur and interact with each other, cogitative and emotional processing. Cognitive components relate to beliefs about illness and emotional relate to feelings about illness. The stages and components interact with each other as shown in figure 3. For example, appraisal of the coping mechanism employed will affect future interpretation of the illness. The model is self regulatory because the individual's actions are aiming to regulate themselves to maintain a desired state of health.

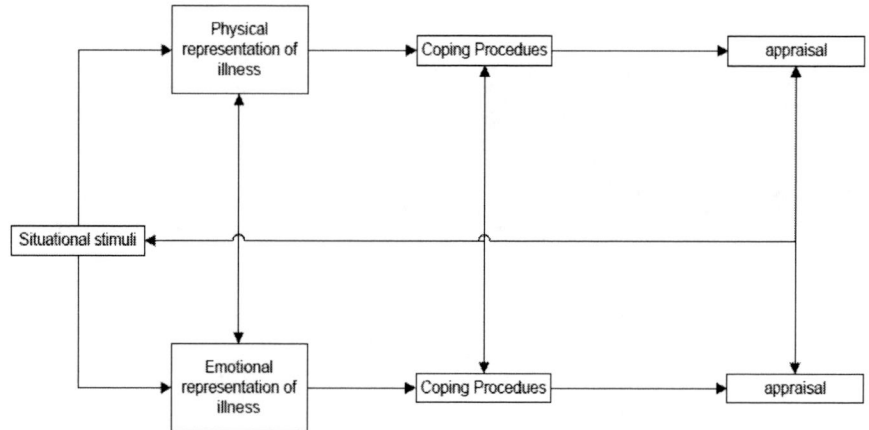

Leventhal,H. & Difenbach, M. (1992).

Figure 3. Self Regulatory Model.

Adherence interventions that work within the self regulatory model can act at any of the three stages. They make seek to influence individuals' interpretation of illness through health education, their choice of coping strategy and patients' assessment of the effects of treatment or other coping strategies tried.

The Transtheoretical Stages of Change Model (Proschaska, & Diclemente 1992)

The transtheoretical model of change (Proschaska, & Diclemente 1992) differs from other models, as its focus is an individual's motivation to adhere to a health promoting behaviour or treatment regime rather than their health beliefs and emotions. The model identified five stages which an individual may be at in relation to adhering to a particular health behaviour or treatment regime. First, at the precontemplation stage, an individual has no intention to adhere in next six months. Second, at the contemplation stage, an individual is considering adhering in the next 6 months but has not yet made a commitment to doing so. Third, at the preparation stage an individual has made a commitment to adhering to treatment in the next month. Fourth, at the action stage, an individual is actively adhering to treatment but has been doing so for less than six months. Finally, at the maintenance stage an individual has been adhering to treatment for over 6 months.

Interventions within the framework of the transtheoretical model will be tailored to the stage of change which an individual is currently at. For example, an individual who has not considered adherence treatment, may be given information about the benefits of changing, whereas patients at the action stage may need support in assessing the effects of treatment. Motivational interviewing is an intervention based on the stages of changes model. This is a strategy where patients are encouraged to assess the situation and find reasons to motivate themselves to adhere to treatment rather than simply be provided with healthcare information.

A tool for monitoring adherence according the the transtheoretical model has been developed and validated (Willey et al., 2000).

CONTEMPORARY MODELS

Whilst the psychological models have taken a broader approach to adherence than the traditional biomedical model, they have limitations and have not been good at predicting actual behaviour in linear regression models (Barber 2005). They are designed to be predictive of intentional non-adherence but not unintentional non adherence. In addition, they focus on the patient alone and not their interaction with the healthcare system. These issues have been addressed by more contemporary approaches, including the accident causation framework and concordance/shared decision making approaches.

The Accident Causation Framework (Reason 1990, Vincent et al. 1998)

The theory of causation of human error (Reason 1990, Vincent et al., 1998) is widely used to understand medical errors healthcare and has been used to explain causes of medication errors made by healthcare professionals (Dean et al., 2002, Taxis & Barber 2003). More recently, it has been ultilised to understand patients' adherence to taking prescribed medication (Barber 2005) and it is also potentially relevant to adherence to other types of treatment.

Firstly, human error theory classifies non adherence or errors in medication taking into 4 types: slips, lapses, mistakes and violations. Slips and lapses are unintentional and occur when an individual intends to do something but the action is not executed. Lapses are memory failures, such as forgetting to take medication. Slips occur when the action is executed incorrectly such as intending to take one medication, but taking another instead. Mistakes occur when a person wants to achieve something but uses the wrong plan or rule to achieve it. Mistakes may occur when patients are not informed or do not understand the information given by healthcare providers such the need to take a new medication in addition to, and not instead of medication already prescribed (Barber 2005). Finally violations are deliberate acts of non adherence. Violations are equivalent to intentional non adherence. The individual makes an informed decision to be non adherent based on their health beliefs, motivations and experiences.

Secondly, human error theory identifies error producing conditions which would make it more likely that an error would occur. Non-adherence is therefore seen as predominantly a system issue rather than one of personal blame (Barber, 2005). From this point of view, when attempting to understand the causes of non adherence both the individual and the system, or context in which the individual operates, need to be considered. Reason's (1990) organisational accident model incorporates both individual and system factors and has been adapted into a framework specific to healthcare by Vincent et al. (1998). Vincent et al., (1998) created a framework for the analysis of adverse events and critical incidents in healthcare. The framework considers the following factors when assessing the causes and contributory factors of each incident: the patient's characteristics, including their medical conditions and their beliefs about the necessity and concerns about treatment; actions of individual healthcare staff involved; the nature and complexity of the task itself; the environment in which they live; communication with others; and the organisational factors that influence other conditions, such as policy and economic decisions and underlying culture.

From the human error theory angle, non-adherence is considered a symptom, rather than a diagnosis and in order to target adherence services to support patients' needs, it is necessary to diagnose the cause. Intentional and unintentional non-adherence have different underlying causes and require different interventions which need to be tailored towards individuals rather than using one size fit all approaches. For example, lapses of memory may be addressed by reminders, slips by using monitored dosing systems which aid patients by compartmentalising medication in dosage times, mistakes by healthcare education and violations by attempting to influence beliefs or by adjusting regimes to better fit lifestyle. The error producing conditions also need to be assessed and considered. For example, on an individual level the complexity of administering inhalers could be addressed by changing to a less complex inhaler device and on an organisational level, an underlying change in the culture of communication between patients and healthcare professional may reduce non-adherence.

A tool for monitoring adherence in line with the accident causation framework has been developed and validated (Garfield et al., 2012). This allows for the classification of adherence as intentional or non intentional and for the continuous monitoring of non adherence to measure the effects of interventions and inform future treatment.

Concordance/Shared Decision-Making

Concordance and shared decision making are not synonymous with adherence but are included here as a relevant contemporary approach to treatment decisions. Further to the development of the understanding that patients are actively involved in making decisions about their medicines, there has been increasing recognition that patients should work in partnership to decide upon treatment strategies. This is known as shared decision making or concordance. For example, in Great Britain, The Royal Pharmaceutical Society of Great Britain launched the initiative from compliance to concordance in 1997 (RPSGB & MSD1997). Concordance has been defined as' a new approach to the prescribing and taking of medicines. It is an agreement reached after negotiation between a patient and a healthcare professional that respects the beliefs and wishes of the patient in determining whether, when and how medicines are to be taken. Although reciprocal, this is an alliance in which the healthcare professionals recognise the primacy of the patient's decisions about taking the recommend medications.' The shared decision making/ concordance model recognises that patients and healthcare professionals have their own areas of expertise and need to work together. Whereas clinicians possess medical knowledge, patients understand their experience of illness and their values and priorities in its management.

This model also recognises that not all patients will wish to take an active part in decision making. If patients wish the responsibility for decision making to be made by the healthcare professional that is considered as the patient's decision. Whilst, age, gender, social class, clinical condition and type of decision (Garfield 2007, Say 2006) have been associated with preferences for involvement in decision making, these factors only explain a small proportion of the variability. Therefore establishing individual's preferences is an important part of the shared decision making/ concordance model.

Interventions to increase concordance will aim to focus on communication skills training for healthcare professionals, couching for patients and decision aids (Coulter 2006). The latter are tools designed to help patients to identify their values and preferences, weigh up the risks and benefits of treatment options and to be used in combination with interaction with healthcare professionals.

Tools have been developed for monitoring the extent to which healthcare professionals involve patients in decisions within clinical consultations (Elywn et al., 2003).

Conclusion

A large number of models of adherence to medical treatment have been developed. The underlying theoretical approach taken will affect the type of intervention employed to monitor and reduce non adherence.

References

Ajzen I. (1991). The theory of planned behavior. Organizational and behavior. *Organizational behavior and human decision process. 50*, 179-211.

Bandura, A. (1977). Self efficacy: towards a unifying theory of behavioral change. Psychological Review, 84, 191-215.

Barber, N. Safdar, A. and Franklin, B.(2005). Can human error theory explain non-adherence? *Pharmacy World and Science 27*, 300-304.

Becker, M.H.(1994). The health belief model and personal health behaviour. *Health Education Monographs 2*, 324-508.

Coulter, A Ellins J. (2006). Patient focussed interventions. A review of the evidence. London: (The Picker Institute).

Dean, B.S., Schachter, M, Vincent, C. and Barber, N. (2002) Prescribing errors in hospital inpatients—incidence and clinical significance. *Quality and Safety in Health Care* 11, 340–4.

Elwyn, G., Edwards, A., Wensing M, Hood K., Atwell C. and Grol, R. (2003). Shared decision making: developing the OPTION scale for measuring patient involvement. *Quality and Safety in Health Care*, 12, 93-9.

Garfield, S., Smith, F., Francis, S.A. and Chalmers, C. (2007) Can patients' preferences for involvement in decision-making regarding the use of medicines be predicted? *Patient Education and Counseling 66*, 31-370.

Garfield, S., Eliasson, L., Clifford, S., Willson, A. and Barber, N. (2012). Developing the Diagnostic Adherence to Medication Scale (the DAMS) for use in clinical practice, *BMC Health Services Research 12*, 350.

Leventhal, H. and Difenbach, M. (1992). Illness cognition: using common sense to understand treatment adherence and affect cognition interactions. *Cognitive Therapy and Research 16*, 143-163.

Proschaska, J.O. and Diclemente, C.C. (1992). Stages of change in the modification of problem behaviours. *Programme of behaviour modification 2*, 183-218.

Reason, J. (1990). *Human error.* Cambridge: University of Cambridge.

Rosenstock, I. (1974).Historical origins of the Health Belief Model *Health Education Monographs 2*, 1-8.

Rotter, J.R. (1996). Generalised expectancies for internal versus external control of reinforcement. *Psychological Monographs* 81, 1-28.

RPSGB and Merck Sharp Dohme (1997) *From compliance to concordance: achieving shared goals in medicine taking,* London: RPSGB.

Say, R. Murtagh, M. and Thompson, R. (2006). Patients' preference for involvement in medical decision making: A narrative review. *Patient Education and Counseling 60, 102-114.*

Taxis, K. and Barber, N. (2003). Causes of intravenous medication errors: an ethnographic study. *Quality and Safety in Health Care 12*, 343–7.

Vincent C, Taylor-Adams, S.E. and Stanhope, N. (1998). Framework for analysing risk and safety in clinical practice. *BMJ 316*, 1154–7.

Wallston, K.A., Wallston B.S. and Devellis R. (1978). *Development of multi dimensional health locus of control. Health Education Monographs 6,* 160-170.

Willey, C., Redding, C., Stafford, J., Garfield, F., Geletko, S., Flanigan, T., Melbourne, K., Mitty J, C.J. (2000) Stages of change for adherence with medication regimens for chronic disease: Development and validation of a measure. *Clinical Therapeutics 22,* 858-871.

In: Adherence to Treatment in Clinical Practice   ISBN: 978-1-63117-841-2
Editor: Pamela Lofland   © 2014 Nova Science Publishers, Inc.

Chapter 3

CLINICAL IMPLICATIONS OF ADHERENCE TO TREATMENT OF PATIENTS WITH SOCIAL ANXIETY

Mariângela Gentil Savoia[*] *and Silvia Sztamfater*
Anxiety Clinic of Institute of Psychiatry, University of São Paulo, Brasil

ABSTRACT

Background: Adherence to treatment is a relevant factor able to influence results obtained by clinical trials and clinical practice. The components of adherence can be considered by the actions of patients, professionals, family and social support programs. Concerning mental health disorders, nonadherence is related to poorer treatment outcomes, such as: lack of symptom stabilization, homelessness, lower quality of life and hospitalization.

Purpose: This chapter aims to discuss adherence to treatment to social anxiety disorder and possible interventions to increase adherence.

Results: It was found that some patients on a social phobia research had a poor adherence to group psychotherapy, some of them having abandoned therapy at different stages. The results showed that those patients had a history of poor adherence to other treatments, a misunderstanding of their treatment outcomes and clinical status, lack of

---

[*] Corresponding author: Mariangela Gentil Savoia, Ipq – Hospital das Clínicas FMUSP, AMBAN – Programa Ansiedade, R. Dr. Ovídio Pires de Campos, 785, Cep: 05403-010, São Paulo, SP, Brasil, Fone-fax: 5511 3069.6988, E-mail: mangy.savoia@globo.com.

motivation and attribution of their symptoms to personality features instead of the disease. Yet, a correlation between depression and active treatment was found (SSRI, CBT or combined). The patients with dependent personality trait adhered less to treatment. The antisocial and borderline disorders were correlated with low adherence in CBT. The presence or absence of social abilities before treatment was not related to adherence, different from what we found in the literature. Besides, social phobic patients adherence to treatment is likely to increase when family members also participate in the intervention.

Conclusion: Therapists should be concerned to patient's motivation and with his/her continuous evaluation of adherence in order to detect those who most likely would abandon the treatment in order to prevent patients, initially motivated, discouraged with the treatment and consequently leaving. The findings of personality disorders indicate the need to deal with these disorders before or concomitant the treatment of social phobia. A possible solution to increase adherence to mental disorders patients, particularly anxiety illnesses, is to consider the family as an active and central figure in the patient's treatment. Therefore, adherence interventions that include family as an important variable are likely to succeed.

Keywords: Adherence, anxiety disorders, social phobia, social anxiety, cognitive behavior therapy (CBT), family, psychoeducation

I. Adherence: Discussion of Evidences

Adherence to treatment may be considered as the coincidence degree observed between the patient's behavior and the therapeutic recommendations prescribed by the health care professional (Epstein & Cluss, 1982). Adherence is a relevant factor able to influence results obtained by clinical trials and clinical practice (Savoia & Bernik, 2008).

According to Martin (2013), adherence involves a range of actions including eating (or abstaining from) particular foods, being physically active, undergoing health screenings, keeping health-related appointments and proper taking of medications. The World Health Organization (WHO, 2003) states that the quality of the treatment relationship is an important determinant of adherence; this is why adherence focuses on the collaborative relationship between patients and health care professionals (Martin, Haskard-Zolnierek & DiMatteo, 2010).

On the other hand, it's important to consider some aspects related to nonadherence. It can be expressed in specific behaviors, divided into two categories: behaviors that are never initiated (for example: patients that decide not to follow the medication prescriptions) and behaviors that are abandoned (for example: patients that started a treatment and stopped because of the difficulty) (Martin, 2013). The percentages to nonadherence to treatment vary from 20 to 40% for acute illness, 20 to 60% for chronic illness and 50 to 80% for preventive interventions (Bosworth, 2010). Among children and adolescents, the rate ranges from 43 to 100%, with the mean of 58% in developed countries (Bosworth, 2010) and even lower in the developing world (Martin, 2013). Considering these data, adherence rates are higher among patients with acute conditions compared to patients with chronic diseases (Martin, 2013). Furthermore, rates of adherence are influenced by multiple factors, including the history, beliefs and expectations of the patient, symptoms associated with the disease, treatment's side effects, the complexity of the treatment regimen and social factors such as financial burden and family pressure (Martin, 2013).

Osterberg & Blaschke (2005) state that physicians` ability to recognize nonadherence to treatment is poor, which contributes to increase the unsatisfactory health outcomes, lower quality of life and health care costs.

Although health professionals face a high level of poor or nonadherence to treatment, there are potential solutions that may reduce this situation. These solutions involve simple strategies such as: establish a therapeutic relationship and trust, identify the patient's concerns, take into account the patient's preferences, explain the benefits of the treatment options, minimize adverse effects, provide support, encouragement and follow up (Mitchell & Selmes, 2007).

The components of adherence can be considered by the actions of patients, professionals, family and social support programs. Concerning the patients, the actions are those involving their level of knowledge and skills to cope with the treatment. Yet, to the professional, the clear communication about the expected patients behaviors in certain condition or context and the characteristics of the disease, chronic or acute, which relates time and excused investment in specific treatments. The issues relating to family, social support network in which the patient is inserted, the structure of public health and health promotion and prevention policies can facilitate or hinder services, responses of adherence (DiMatteo, 2004).

The problem of nonadherence has been much discussed, but has been relatively neglected in the mainstream delivery of primary care health services.

Despite an extensive knowledge base, efforts to address the problem have been fragmented, and with few exceptions have failed to harness the potential contributions of the diverse health disciplines. A stronger commitment to a multidisciplinary approach is needed in order to make progress in this area. This will require coordinated action from health professionals, researchers, health planners and policy-makers (WHO, 2003, p.24).

Adherence from the Perspective of Mental Health Treatment

Nonadherence among psychiatric patients is related to poorer treatment outcomes, such as: lack of symptom stabilization, homelessness, lower quality of life and hospitalization (Magura et al., 2013). In general, the psychiatric treatment's goals are different from the usual ones, as many psychiatric patients present a particularly difficult adherence because of the poor mental health that influences the understanding, memory, motivation and attitudes towards the treatment adherence (Haskard-Zolnierek & Williams, 2013). In those cases, the average adherence rate is 58% (Cramer & Rosenheck, 1998). In the same way, Gonzales et al. (2005) suggest that between 55% and 60% of primary care patients don't take psychiatric medications as described and fail to follow the treatment. According to the authors, the usual reason for medication nonadherence in this context is medication side effects. Others researches also emphasize that patients are more nonadherent if they have the following profile: unmarried, male, young adult, belong to a lower economic level, have a history of nonadherence, perceive they don't need psychiatric care, have an uncertain diagnosis and ambiguous sympton (Gonzales et al., 2005).

Another relevant aspect related to mental health adherence is the knowledge that primary care physicians have about mental health disorders. It's known that depression has been considered as the most common clinical problem that primary care physicians need to diagnose and treat. However, those physicians fail to diagnose as many as 50%-70% of patient who present depressive disorder. Even when depression is diagnosed, it's treated accurately only 30%-40% of the time (Martin et al., 2005). Therefore, the opportunity to deal with a common factor of nonadherence is missed in this scenario.

It's important to mention that mental disorders that have chronic evolution can be characterized by instability in the treatment, alternating moments of improvement and worsening. Improvements are possible due to medication and non-medication treatments such as psychotherapy, psychoeducation, family therapy, occupational therapy, home visits among others (Cardoso & Galera, 2009).

Concerning the medication treatment, Osterberg & Blaschke (2005) observe that half of patients with major depression stop taking antidepressants three months after the beginning of therapy. The mean rate of adherence among those with depression is 65% according to the authors. Cardoso & Galera (2006) conducted a data base search in Medline and Pubmed and found that there is no difference of adherence among typical or atypical antipsychotics. Also concluded that 40% of the patients treated with conventional neuroleptics stopped the medication during the first year of treatment and 75% stopped taking within 2 years. Yet, Osterberg & Blaschke (2005) report that patients with schizophrenia present rates of adherence between 50% and 60%. Related to bipolar disorder, Osterberg & Blaschke (2005) state that the rates are as low as 35%. Likewise, Sejatovic et al. (2007) examined adherence with lithium and anticonvulsant medication among patients with bipolar disorder and deduced that nearly one in two individuals did not take their medications as prescribed. Given this reality, psychiatric patients have great difficulty to follow a medication regimen; however, they also have the greatest potential for benefiting from adherence (Osterberg & Blaschke 2005).

Among the reasons reported by the psychiatric patients to justify the non adherence, are: disease denial, missed medication, lack of control over his/her own life, medication adverse effects, forgetfulness, euphoria absence (in bipolar disorder patients) and the belief in the disease's spontaneous resolution (Kech, 1998).

Yet, non-medication treatments to improve adherence are relevant as studies established significant correlation between social support with patient adherence to medical regimens (DiMatteo, 2004). According to the author, meta-analyses establish significant average effect sizes between adherence and practical, emotional and social support, such as: family cohesiveness and conflict, marital status and living arrangement of adults. Some datas: adherence is 1,74 times higher in patients from cohesive families and 1,53 times lower in patients from families in conflict. Besides, data from the scientific literature show that psychological interventions, such as cognitive behavior therapy and family therapy, improve compliance with drug treatment and the gains persist over time (Katon et al., 1996; Kemp et al., 1996; Barlow et al., 2000; Pilling et al., 2002; Craske et al., 2005). Even improving adherence, nonadherence to treatment has been found to be high in psychotherapy, with premature treatment dropout rates ranging from 30 to 60% (Wierzbicki & Pekarik, 1993).

The scenario of nonadherence among mental health patients complicates because of stigma. People who would benefit from mental health treatments opt not to seek any kind; to avoid the label of "mentally ill" and the harm it brings. Stigma causes 2 kinds of harm that may complicate treatment participation: it impairs self-esteem and deviate people of social opportunities (Corrigan, 2004). The researcher complements that less than 30% of people with psychiatric disorders seek treatment.

Situations that worsen adherence are that require a long time of treatment, the situations that have a preventive nature, or even when the patient's lifestyle is affected. Changes in lifestyle are the hardest treatments to follow (Monteiro, 2001).

Summarizing, assuming that in the last decades psychiatric treatment has undergone many changes and developed a new organizational structure for mental health care, the results in primary care are worrying, as physicians have difficulties to diagnose and treat mental health disorders. These changes aforementioned are related to deinstitutionalization of treatment and to consider the patient actively in his own treatment. In other words, patients are encouraged to collaborate with mental health professionals in order to improve treatment goals; they can become the most important agents of change for themselves (Mueser et al., 2002).

The characteristics of healthy behavior, health maintenance and changes in lifestyle are issues that can be covered by general principles of behavior (Mejias, 1984).

And What about Adherence to Anxiety Disorders Treatment?

Anxiety disorders can be considered as illnesses that compromise quality of life and psychosocial functioning. In other words, people with anxiety disorders present significant functional and occupational impairments. Besides, anxiety disorders patients use public health services more often, increasing medical costs (Lanouette & Stein, 2010; Santana & Fontenelle, 2011). Among mental disorders, anxiety disorders are the most common class, affecting up to 28,8% of the general population at some point during their lives (Lanouette & Stein, 2010; Santana & Fontenelle, 2011; Taylor et al., 2012).

Patients with diagnosis of panic disorder, Monteiro (2001) stated that 83,3% failed to perform at least one of the expected behaviors during the treatment. The author proposed an intervention grounded in educational and behavioral strategies, which adherence rate varied inversely with the number of drugs prescribed, the number of doses per day, and the number of activities prescribed for treatment.

Concerning the treatments, there are empirically supported therapies (pharmacological and nonpharmacological) for these disorders, such as serotonin reuptake inhibitors (SRIs) and Cognitive Behavior Therapy (CBT); although the evidence suggests that these disorders in many patients, possibly even 50-60%, remain symptomatic despite these first line treatments. Other patients find it difficult to tolerate or adhere to treatment and dropout prematurely (Lanouette & Stein, 2010; Taylor et al., 2012).

Normally, studies of CBT or SRIs last 10-12 weeks of treatment. For this period, meta-analyses of anxiety disorders reported dropout rates from 9-21% (M=16%) for CBT and 18-30% (M=24%) for SRIs. The proportion of nonresponders ranged from 34-36% for CBT (M=35%) and 30% for SRIs (based on a single meta-analysis). Another study focused on drug treatments for anxiety disorders concluded that approximately 50% of patients were not significantly improved after 6-16 months of treatment and the complete recovery was uncommon (Taylor et al., 2012).

Related to CBT dropout, Taylor et al. (2012) assume that there are motivational factors involved, such as: low motivation for treatment, poor readiness for change, low treatment credibility, poor therapeutic alliance, patient preference for alternative treatments and practical barriers (for example: transportation problems). Associated to SRIs, the most common reason for dropping out is treatment side effects, although in this area more researches are needed. Other important data from a recent meta-analysis of a variety of disorders, including also anxiety disorders, showed that treatment trials that included systematic therapeutic homework were associated with better outcomes. Following this perspective, studies focused particularly on anxiety disorders found the same results (Taylor et al., 2012).

Santana & Fontenelle (2011) add that cognitive variables may be an important intervention factor because they are easier to change than clinical and sociodemographic variables. Thus, treatment programs need to consider these expectations and include structured interventions to motivate patients in treatment even before it begins.

II. OLD INTERVENTIONS: NEW FINDINGS

Up to know we discussed the concept of adherence and the impacts on mental health field, focusing on anxiety disorders as well. At this point, our goal is to revisit options that probably would increase adherence. Revisit means to examine again some interventions that had already been studied by researchers in the past; however, based on new findings, these interventions would be readapted and produce new outcomes.

Thus, this section is divided into some parts in order to make a review of a particularly variable, family, and its influence in treatments of mental health disorders, giving special attention to anxiety disorders and a particular class: social anxiety (or social phobia).

Family Insertion into Psychiatric Pathologies

Since the beginning of the last century, the relation between family and mental illness has been studied. In 1921, several analyses were directed towards the influence of psychopathology on family functioning. However, it was only at the end of the 1950s and first years of 1960 that more in-depth studies were carried out in order to elucidate the impact caused by a member's mental illness on the family. At the end of 1980, studies were intensified by the developing of DSM III and DSM III-R criteria (Lange et al., 1993). Besides, the deinstitutionalization of psychiatric treatment, changes occurred in the patient's rehabilitation, such as the family's role as a central figure in this process.

Given this scenario, approximately 50% to 90% of psychiatric patients live within their family environment (Lauber et al., 2001) and as a consequence, the usual family caregiver member may also be affected by his/her responsibilities and come to suffer negative mental effects as anxiety, depression, fear, and guilt in addition to difficult communication with the patient (Pickett-Schenk et al., 2006; Rossler, 2006). By having a daily contact with the psychiatric patient, family members should be able to report their acquired knowledge at assisting that type of patient; unfortunately, caregivers have very few opportunities to exchange their experiences with the attending multiprofessional team, and also, usually have to be submitted to a frustrating and disorderly interaction with the mental care services (Hatfiled, 1978; Pickett-Schenk et al., 2006). Many times, the professional/caregiver interactional success is impaired by the lacking attention given to the caregivers reports on their experience; however, some studies state that interventions which do not consider the caregivers specific needs are not as effective as those that facilitate the means to deal with those needs (Pollio, 1998).

At present, the psychiatric rehabilitation goal aims to help chronic patients in developing their emotional, intellectual and social abilities in order to be prepared for life in society. When reaching this stage, patients should have the capability to work or study but also have a free access to professional help whenever necessary. Lately, the paradigm health-disease underwent a number of changes regarding the psychiatric pathologies field in which chronic patients previously considered as incapacitated are seen today as dysfunctional individuals in need of professional and family support in his/her readaptation to social life (Rossler, 2006). Thus, adequate measures as instructing and training psychoeducational groups about mental health must include family members and caregivers since the results attained by this type of education will not be successful enough without their involvement in the patient's rehabilitation process.

Psychoeducation and Family: Present Overview and Social Anxiety Patient's Perspectives

It was possible to observe that there had been a number of improvements in rehabilitation programs for the psychiatric patient to be reinserted into society. This movement is based in the family as an active and central figure in the patient's readaptation.

A new developmental technique - psychoeducational family intervention - strives to meet the needs of both patient and family. The psychoeducation technique was first applied to schizophrenic patients' caregivers and since the 1990s its use was expanded to the treatment of other pathologies as the bipolar syndrome and depression cases. Several psychoeducational programs were developed in the last two decades directed towards family members and caregivers in different formats as time duration, training location, type of approach and participation form: individual family, family groups, or both possibilities alternately (Dixon et al., 2001).

This intervention is intended to teach the caregiver about aspects and procedures related to the psychiatric patient's treatment, developing capacity, expected abilities, prevention of the relapse of the disease, problem solving strategies and harmonious companionship (Dixon et al., 2001). Studies carried out in different countries show that psychoeducation provides the caregivers with higher satisfaction levels, decreases the family burden, promotes the patient's higher adherence and acceptance of treatment, reduces the caregiver's preoccupation and frustration and decreases levels of relapses and rehospitalization (Sherman, 2003; Dixon et al., 2004; Lukens & McFarlane, 2004; Pickett-Schenk et al., 2006).

Anxiety disorders although chronic and incapacitating nature, and high levels of incidence in the population, the number of studies concerning family participation and impacting support when dealing with the anxiety disorders patients are still scarce. However, research findings related to compulsive-obsessive symptoms and post-traumatic stress (Kalra et al., 2008) confirm that family participation is effective in those patients' treatment (Diamond & Josephson, 2005). Even with proven evidence that this type of intervention is shown to be effective in anxiety disorders, other pathologies related to this disorder, as for example the social phobia syndrome, are still disregarded (Kalra et al., 2008).

Given all these considerations, the support of family members is currently the most important factor to facilitate recovery of the psychiatric patient. This support can be given through the participation of the family in psychoeducational programs, for which scientific studies proved to be consistent for this purpose (Dixon et al., 2001).

In a systematic review that examined the relation between family psychoeducation and mental disorders, data revealed expressive difference between studies carried out with schizophrenic patients and families when compared to other pathologies. According to those findings, a reasonable number of investigations approaching bipolar disorders are likely to be found, while when considering anxiety disorders, a larger concentration of studies related to compulsive-obsessive disorders are reported (Sztamfater & Savoia, in press).

Regarding social anxiety, data showed a very small amount of studies approaching family participation in children and adolescent's treatment but no study approaching family participation in adult patient's illness. Only one similar study (Fisher et al., 2004) was found but it solely described the systematization of performed investigations on adolescent anxiety disorders, and at the same time, emphasized the importance for family doctors to correctly evaluate, diagnose and treat anxiety disorders involving avoidance and opposition behaviors in adolescent individuals (Sztamfater & Savoia, in press).

Treatment Adherence to Social Anxiety Disorder

Social phobia is a psychiatric disorder affected by several factors related to low adherence levels, common to general disease occurrences and treatments indicated below. In addition to those "universal" factors, there are also factors related to different psychiatric diseases and most importantly to disease peculiarities as social contact avoidance, which may render difficulties for the therapist-patient interaction. Thus, the analysis off the adherence to social phobia treatment is extremely relevant when dealing with this disorder.

Some studies tried to identify which factors could be associated to the higher levels of nonadherence to treatment in social phobia patients, either during treatment or in the follow up period. No compliance differences were observed concerning patients disorder severity, however, patients presenting avoidance personality traits showed to be less responsive to the therapeutic process, while the more dependent patients tried diligently to carry out their homework tasks, paranoids patient's tendency was to leave exposition tasks unfinished (Edelman & Chambless, 1989). The specific social phobia subtype obtained significant better results than the generalized subtype in treatment compliance, withdrawing rate, and improved status following the treatment (Turner et al., 1994). Social skills may be related to those patient's adherence to treatment while social phobic patients generally present deficits which impair their relationship with the therapeutic team (Savoia & Vianna, 2011). Another eventual factor associated to the patient's low adherence level to treatment may be assigned to the presence of comorbidity with depression (Van Ameringen et al., 1991).

In our research group we developed some researches in this line.

The first one was a qualitative essay. It was found that some patients on a social phobia research had a poor adherence to group psychotherapy, some of them having abandoned therapy at different stages. There were two different groups of patients, some abandoning treatment even before its beginning, and others doing it during its course of 16 weeks. Patients who abandoned therapy were interviewed in order to determine which factors had a negative influence on their adherence. The results showed that those patients had a history of poor adherence to other treatments, a misunderstanding of their treatment outcomes and clinical status, lack of motivation and attribution of their symptoms to personality features instead of the disease (Malerbi et al., 2000).

Following this line of research we decided to identify the predictor factors which related with social phobia in a clinical trial witch studied the impact of four kinds of treatment. Pharmacological treatment with selective serotonin reuptake (SSRI), cognitive behavior therapy (CBT), combined treatment (SSRI and CBT) and placebo in 144 social phobia patients. This way was possible to estimate the probability of one individual diagnosed with social phobia, to adhere to these treatments. Based on the treatments findings a correlation between depression and active treatment was found (SSRI, CBT or combined), the patients with dependent personality trait adhered less to treatment. The antisocial and borderline disorders were correlated with low adherence in CBT. The presence or absence of social abilities before treatment was not related to adherence, different from what we found in the literature (Savoia & Bernik, 2008).

Considering that several clinical studies on adult social phobic patients have been developed lately, the related literature fails to present studies of interventionist nature dealing with family participation in the patient's treatment, Sztamfater & Savoia (2010) developed a study including 15 male and 15 female patients affected by social phobia, age range 25 to 40 years, and showing depressed mood; eight caregivers were also included in the study. Instruments used for the study were: the Structured clinical interview for DSM-IV (SCID), Social avoidance and distress scale (SAD), Fear of negative evaluation scale (FNE) and Social skills questionnaire (EMES-M). Family members answered to the adapted Burden interview scale. Three CBT therapy groups were formed and each one included ten patients that attended 20 weekly 90-minutes sessions. Caregivers' attendance was fortnightly carried out with ten one- hour sessions CBT group. Data showed that twelve patients were able to conclude the program; ten participants quit the ongoing program; eight patients were present at the initial interview only. After the intervention, nine participants showed SAD and FNE decreased scores; two patients showed decreased FNE scores; and increased scores in both scales were observed in one patient. All the participants who had family members included in the program concluded the intervention. Statistical analysis showed significant mean differences between SAD and FNE scales after the procedure.

This study showed that social phobic patients adherence to treatment is likely to increase when family members also participate in the intervention.

Implications for the Therapeutic Management

This section corresponds to ours and the literature findings about the topic of adherence in social phobic patients.

Adherence should not be considered as a characteristic or trait inherent to the patient's personality, but accepted as a cluster of several different self-care behaviors (Glasgow, 1985). This would be a type of modeled behavior and maintained by its consequences; in this way, it is easier to understand why a treatment offers a symptomatic relief associated to the highest levels of adherence, since prevention actions are associated to future complications, issues that can be covered by general principles of behavior.

Some intervention procedures are recommended in order to improve adherence, such as patient's education about their disease and the treatments; providing patients with objective markers for their improvements; the therapist should emphasize objective aspects of the improvements in order to suit the patient's perception to the therapeutic evolution presented in his/her little progress. Therapists should be concerned to patient's motivation and with his/her continuous evaluation of adherence in order to detect those who most likely would abandon the treatment in order to prevent patients, initially motivated, discouraged with the treatment and consequently leaving.

In the other hand the depressive patients require active intervention, pharmacological or CBT, or combined. The patients with personality trait of dependence of reward adhered less to all treatments, indicating the need for changes in this factor for engaging the patient to treatment. The findings of personality disorders indicate the need to deal with these disorders before or concomitant the treatment of social phobia.

A possible solution to increase adherence to mental disorders patients, particularly anxiety illnesses, is to consider the family as an active and central figure in the patient's treatment. Therefore, adherence interventions that include family as an important variable are likely to succeed.

CONCLUSION

Those studies show the importance of the evaluation of the adherence to the various aspects of disease characteristics. Each disease should indicate the important elements to be considered for the most effective approach. In our researches about social anxiety we suggested specific interventions to this disorder.

Adherence to treatment seems to be a field to promising studies for CBT, which is a theoretical approach that is based primarily on studies of processes and methods of the learning area, emphasizing the importance of helping individuals to build new or strengthen appropriate behavioral repertoires already acquired (Moraes et al., 2009)

Finally it is important to highlight that effective strategies employed in certain patients, may be ineffective for others, so it becomes necessary to evaluate strategies for each patient.

REFERENCES

Barlow, D. H. et al. (2000). Cognitive behavior therapy, imipramine, or their combination for panic disorder: a randomized controlled trial. *JAMA: the journal of the American Medical Association, 283*, 2529-2536.

Bosworth, H. (2010). Introduction. In H. Bosworth (Ed.). *Improving patient treatment adherence: a clinician's guide.* New York: Springer.

Craske, M. G. et al. (2005). Does the addition of cognitive behavioral therapy improve panic disorder treatment outcome relative to medication alone in primary-care setting? *Psychological Medicine, 35*(11), 1645-1654.

Cramer, J. A. & Rosenheck. R. (1998). Compliance with medication regimens for mental and physical disorders. *Psychiatric Services, 49*(2), 196-201.

Cardoso, L. & Galera, S. A. F. (2006). Adesão ao tratamento psicofarmacológico. *Acta Paulista de Enfermagem, 19*(3), 343-348.

Cardoso, L. & Galera, S. A. F. (2009). Mental patients and their profile of compliance with psychopharmacological treatment. *Revista da Escola de Enfermagem da USP, 43*(1), 161-167.

Corrigan, P. (2004). How stigma interferes with mental health care. *American Psychologist, 59*(7), 614-625.

Diamond, G. & Josephson, A. (2005). Family-based treatment research: a 10-year update. *Journal of the American Academy of Child & Adolescent Psychiatry, 44*(9), 872-887.

DiMatteo, M. R. (2004). Variations in patients' adherence to medical recommendations: a quantitative review of 50 years of research. *Medical Care, 42*(3), 200-209.

Dixon, L. et al. (2001). Evidence-based practices for services to families of people with psychiatric disabilities. *Psychiatric Services, 52*(7), 903-910.

Dixon, L. et al. (2004). Outcomes of the peer-taught 12-week family-to-family education program for severe mental illness. *Acta Psychiatrica Scandinavica, 109*(3), 207-215.

Edelman, R. & Chambless. D. (1989). Adherence during sessions and homework in cognitive-behavioral group treatment of social phobia. *Behaviour Research and Therapy, 33*(5), 573-577.

Epstein, L. A., Cluss, P. A. (1982). A behavioral medicine perspective on adherence to long term medical regimens. *Journal of Consulting Clinical Psychology, 50*(6), 950-71.

Fisher, P. H. et al. (2004). Skills for social and academic success: a school-based intervention for social anxiety disorder in adolescents. *Clinical Child and Family Psychology Review, 7*(4), 241-249.

Glasgow, R. E. et al. (1985). Regimen aherence a problematic construct in diabetes reserach. *Diabetes Care, 8930*, 300-301.

Gonzales, J. et al. (2005). Adherence to mental health treatment in a primary care clinic. *The Journal of The American Board of Family Practice, 18*(2), 87-96.

Haskard-Zolnierek, K. B. & Williams, S. (2013). Adherence and health behavior change in the context of mental health challenges. In L. R. Martin & M. R. DiMatteo (Eds.). *The Oxford handbook of health communication, behavior change, and treatment adherence.* New York: Oxford University Press.

Hatfield, A. B. (1978). Psychological costs of schizophrenia to the family. *Social Work, 23*(5), 355-359.

Kalra, H. et al. (2008). Caregiver burden in anxiety disorders. *Current Opinion in Psychiatry, 21*(1), 70-73.

Katon, W. et al. (1996). A multifaceted intervention to improve treatment of depression in primary care. *Archives of General Psychiatry, 53*, 924-932.

Keep, P. et al. (1998). Factors associated with pharmacological non-compliance inpatients with mania. *Journal of Clinical Psychiatric, 57*, 292-97.

Kemp, R. et al. (1996). Compliance therapy in psychotic patients: randomised controlled trial. *British Medical Journal, 312*, 345-349.

Lange, A. et al. (1993). Family therapy and psychopatology: developments in research and approaches to treatment. *Journal of Family Therapy, 5*(2), 113-146.

Lanouette, N. M. & Stein, M. B. (2010). Advances in the management of treatment resistant anxiety disorders. *Focus, 8*, 501-524.

Lauber, C. et al. (2001). Lay recommendations on how to treat mental disorders. *Social Psychiatry and Psychiatric Epidemioogic, 36*(11), 553-556.

Lukens, E. P. & McFarlane (2004). Psychoeducation as evidence-based practice: considerations for practice, research, and policy. *Brief Treatment and Crisis Intervention, 4*(3), 205-225.

Magura, S. et al. (2013). Risk factors for medication non-adherence among psychiatric patients with substance misuse histories. *Mental Health and Substance Abuse*, 1-10. doi: 10.1080/17523281.2013.839574

Malerbi, F. K. et al. (2000). A pobre aderência em tratamentos psiquiátricos. *Revista Brasileira de Terapia Comportamental e Cognitiva, 2*(2), 147-155.

Martin, L. R. et al. (2005). The challenge of patient adherence. *Therapeutics and Clinical Risk Management, 1*(3), 189-199.

Martin, L. R., Haskard-Zolnierek, K. B. & DiMatteo, M. R. (2010). *Health behavior change and treatment adherence: evidence-based guidelines for improving healthcare.* New York: Oxford University Press.

Martin, L. R (2013). Barriers and keys to treatment adherence and health behavior change. In L. R. Martin & M. R. DiMatteo (Eds.). *The Oxford handbook of health communication, behavior change, and treatment adherence.* New York: Oxford University Press.

Mejias, N. P. (1984). O psicólogo, a saúde pública e o esforço preventivo. *Revista de Saúde Pública, 18,* 155-161.

Mitchell, A. J. & Selmes, T. (2007). Why don't patients take their medicine? Reasons and solutions in psychiatry. *Advances in Psychiatric Treatment, 13,* 336-346.

Monteiro, M. E. (2001). *Adesão o tratamento psiquiátrico: análise comportamental de pacientes com diagnóstico de transtorno de ansiedade.*(Master's thesis).

Moraes,A.B. et al. (2009) Adherence process from a behavioral analysis perspective. *Revista Brasileira de Terapia Comportamental e Cognitiva, 11,* 271-282.

Mueser, K. T. et al. (2002). Illness management and recovery: a review of the research. *Psychiatric Services, 53*(10), 1272-1284.

Osterberg, L. & Blaschke, T. (2005). Adherence to Medication. *The New England Journal of Medicine, 353*(5), 487-497.

Pickett-Schenk, S. A. et al. (2006). Psychological well-being and relationship outcomes in a randomized study of family-led education. *Archives of General Psychiatry, 63*(9), 1043-1050.

Pilling, S. et al. (2002). Psychological treatments in schizophrenia: I. Meta-analysis of family intervention and cognitive behavior therapy. *Psychological Medicine, 32,* 763-782.

Pollio, D. E. et al. (1998). Content and curriculum in psychoeducation groups for families of persons with severe mental illness. *Psychiatric Services*, *49*(6), 816-822.

Rossler, W. (2006). Psychiatric rehabilitation today: an overview. *World Psychiatry*, *5*(3), 151-157.

Santana, L. & Fontenelle, L. F. (2011). A review of studies concerning treatment adherence of patients with anxiety disorders. *Dove Medical Press*, *5*, 427-439.

Savoia, M. G. & Bernik, M. (2008). Adherence to treatment in social phobia patients: predictors factors. In A. Turley & G. Hofman (Eds.). *Life Style and Health Research Progress*. New York: Nova Publishers Biomedical Books.

Savoia, M. G. & Vianna, A. M. (2011). Especificidades do atendimento a pacientes com transtornos de ansiedade. In M. G. Savoia (Ed.). *A Interface entre Psicologia e Psiquiatria*. 2ª ed. São Paulo: Editora Roca.

Sejatovic, M. et al. (2007). Treatment adherence with lithium and anticonvulsivant medications among patients with bipolar disorder. *Psychiatric Services*, *58*(6), 855-863.

Sherman, M. D. The support and family education (SAFE) program: mental health facts for families. *Psychiatric Services*, *54*(1), 35-37.

Sztamfater, S. & Savoia, M. G. (in press). Treatment of social phobia in adults - considerations regarding family insertion within psychoeducational programs.

Sztamfater, S. & Savoia, M. G. (2010). O impacto da inserção de familiares no tratamento do portador adulto de fobia social. *Acta Medica Portuguesa*, *23*, 25-32.

Taylor, S. et al. (2012). Non-adherence and non-response in the treatment of anxiety disorders. *Journal of Anxiety Disorders*, *26*, 583-589.

Turner, S. M. et al. (1994). Social phobia: a comparison of behavior therapy and atenolol. *Journal of Consulting and Clinical Psychology*, *62*, 350-358.

Van Ameringen, M. et al. (1991). Relationship of social phobia with other psychiatric illness. *Journal of Affective Disorders*, *21*, 93-99.

Wierzbicki, M & Pekarik, G. (1993). A meta-analysis of psychotherapy dropout. *Professional Psychology: Research and Practice*, 24(2), 190-195.

World Health Organization. (2003). *Adherence to long-term therapies: evidence for action*. Geneva, Switzerland: Author. Retrieved January 2014 from http://whqlibdoc.who.int/publications/2003/9241545992.pdf.

In: Adherence to Treatment in Clinical Practice   ISBN: 978-1-63117-841-2
Editor: Pamela Lofland   © 2014 Nova Science Publishers, Inc.

Chapter 4

MOTIVATION AND ADHERENCE IN MANAGEMENT OF CHRONIC PAIN

Zlatka Rakovec-Felser
University of Maribor, Faculty of Medicine,
Department of Health Psychology, Maribor, Slovenia

ABSTRACT

Because acute pain is unpleasant sensory associated with fear and worries it is common reason that somebody seek a medical help. In some cases, even after it has been appropriate treated, it may persist and develop from acute into chronic form. In this article we pay attention to this, to the traditional biomedical treatment generally difficult accessible pain, which significant worse the individual's quality of life. The adherence to treatment, usually combination of pharmacological and physical therapies, we highlighted through individual's changed life position, ways of coping, as well as from the viewpoint of theoretical models, which could predict and explain health behaviour and adherence in medical treatment (e.g., value-expectancy theories as Health belief model, Hochbaum, Rosenstock and Kegels, 1950-88; Bandura's Social cognitive theory, 1977-86; Health Locus of control, Wallston and Wallston, 1982).

After a torment of diagnostic procedures and testing the effects of various available medical options, chronic pain patients could be completely frustrated and deep rooted in a passive, "sick role". Therefore primary goal in psychological treatment as a part of multidimensional, multidisciplinary, and multimodal approach to pain management must be shifting toward interventions emphasizing a proactive and self-management capacity of the patients. But this raises the questions of their motivation. The solutions can be seen in integrative therapeutic approach including the models of provider-patients interactions such as the Motivating Interviewing, MI, (Miller and Rollnick, 1991) and Patient-Centred Model (Stewart et al., 1995) with the principles of Self management concept (Bodenheimer, Lorig et al., 2002; Lorig and Holman, 2003).

Keywords: Chronic pain, quality of life, coping, health beliefs, treatment adherence

INTRODUCTION

As the population rises and life expectancy increases, the prevention and management of chronic disorders becomes an important focus in health care. The majority of chronic disorders are managed with some combination of pharmacotherapy, dietary modification, and/or exercise. Inadequate management contributes to the unnecessary disease progression, and complications, additional doctor visits, hospitalizations, to always new and new inquiries, increasingly aggressive therapeutic measures, and even to the patient's early death. All this has unpleasant implications not only for the individual and his or her family; it is also associated with high costs in public health care system, and finally, affects society as a whole. It became apparent that successfully management is not just a matter of judgment of the physician which therapy, diet or exercise to be used. A major requirement for success is that the patient adheres to prescribed treatment (Dunbar-Jacob, Schlenk, and Caruthers, 2002).

Indeed, in clinical practice the poor or non-adherence is a significant problem and there are several factors that could decrease the level to which an individual follows a recommended health-related or illness-related recommendation. Such influential factors could be not only *the individual differences of chronic patients, the nature of their disease or injury, characteristics of the prescribed treatment regimen,* but also *health-care provider-patient relations, institutions and system of health care, too.* Glasgow and Eakin (1998) have emphasized that self-care is influenced by diverse multilevel factors, including *intrapersonal, social, environmental, and institutional variables* (Gonder-Frederick, Cox, and Clarke, 2002).

Further, we will focuse to the adherence in management of non malignant chronic pain and its specificities. But first, we need to clarify some specificity laid down by complexity of the phenomenon of a pain. What triggers it and what are its effects? In general, we can say that a pain is everyone good known sense that occurs and could becomes a companion on his way ever from birth to his end of the life. Often it is mild and inconsequential, as in the case when we feel a tingling in the legs after keeping them in the same position too long. But, too often it could be intolerable and requires treatment, as in the case of headache due to the brain aneurysm. It could also persists after the healing of the injury, even more, it could becomes chronic, reducing subject's activities and sometimes making his life unbearable (Marchand, 2012).

DEFINITION AND FUNCTIONS OF PAIN

It has been defined as "an unpleasant sensation and emotional experience that is associated with actual or potential tissue damage, or is described in the terms of such damage" (Merskey et al., 1979). However, pain is a phenomenon that cannot be objectively assessed because pain perception is always a subjective experience. Thus, the physician can exactly determine what hurts, how badly, and what the pain feels like only if he listened to the patient's complaints and when he observed his nonverbal behaviour, too. It should be also noted that the perception of pain is always complex and associated with fear. This means that it evokes similar autonomic, cognitive, emotional and behaviour reactions, as we known in this emotion. As the experience of pain individual could overwhelm with anxiety, we should expect that his/her reactions will be the same: the patterns reactions of flight or fight. It is fact that must be taken into account especially during the procedures of the implementation of medical help, particularly when and everywhere the patient participation is needed (Merskey, 1979; Skevington, 2004).

As a symptom of disease or injury a pain can become a major source of individual fears and worries and common reason for seeking a medical care. But pain does not occur only as a result of bodily changes; most often it is a result of reciprocal influence of physical, psychological, and social factors. Because many pains persist after an insult is healed, the ongoing pain rather than the injury underlies the patient's disability (Stucky, Gold, and Xu Zhang, 2001). Its continuous presence contributed to widespread manifestations of suffering, including preoccupation with pain; limitation of personal, social, and work activities; anxiety, demoralization, helplessness, hopelessness, and outright depression; increase use of medications and of health care services; and a generalized adoption of the "sick role", too (Parson, 1958). Moreover, chronic pain not only burden the sufferer, it also undermines the capacity of significant others who provide him or her instrumental or/and emotional support. For example, health care providers could be frustrated as the patient's reports of pain continue, despite their best efforts and absence of pathological basis for pain complaints (Turk and Okifuji, 2002; Turk and Monarch, 2002).

Despite the fact that pain triggers discomfort, and is associated with the individual's suffering, pain sensation could be also useful in many cases. It warns somebody against the dangers in carrying out the daily activities, draws his attention to possible injury or bad health condition, and finally, it informs a doctor or a patient himself about trauma or disease and effectiveness of their treatment. Pain hurts, draws attention, and protects us as *warning message from danger*. It can play an important role in almost all individual's daily activities. Let us remember that we live all the time with minor pains which provide us with low-level feedback *message about our body systems*, information that we then use, often unconsciously, as a basis for making minor adjustments, such as crossing or uncrossing our legs after keeping them in the same position too long. Pain also has important medical consequences. It is the symptom most likely to lead an individual to seek treatment. In the case of failure it may be *a message of healing rates* and as such a important information for physicians. But, the association in both cases is neither simple, nor proportionate. The pain can be also source of misunderstandings between the patients and the medical practitioners. From patient's standpoint, pain may be the problem; to the practitioner, in contrast, pain is a by-product of a disorder (Taylor, 1995).

CLASSIFICATION OF PAIN

As pain is always multidimensional and multimodal phenomenon its classification can be complex. The IASP subcommittee on Taxonomy created in 1986 the first multi-axial system of pain classification. It takes in account *region of body* involved in chronic pain (head, thoracic, abdominal region, etc.), *the affected organ systems* (central nervous system, respiratory and cardiovascular system, musculoskeletal system, gastrointestinal, genitourinary, etc.), *temporal characteristics of pain occurrence* (single episode, recurring irregularly, recurring regularly, etc.), *the duration and intensity of pain* (self-reported as mild, medium or severe; lasting one months or less, 1 months to 6 months, more than 6 months), and *aetiology of pain* – it can be genetic or congenital, induced by trauma or degenerative, etc. (Raj, 2007).

In general, division of pain into two main types is accepted: *acute and chronic pain*. These forms are further divided into *acute, acute recurrent, chronic, chronic recurrent, chronic benign and chronic progressive pain (malignant pain)*. *Acute pain* is usually of less than 6 months in duration, results from some physical injury and disappears when the tissue damage is repaired. While it is going on, acute pain produces substantial anxiety and prompts its sufferer to engage in an urgent search for relief. Once painkillers are administered or the injury begins to heal, the pain and the anxiety disappear (Bond, 1979). An example of such acute pain may be toothache. Acute recurrent pain is more complex. It includes a series of intermittent episodes of pain that are acute in character, but chronic as the condition persists for more than 6 months. Within these types of pain belong for example migraine headache and trigeminal neuralgias.

Chronic pain always begins with acute episode, but does not decrease with treatment and not over time. In its benign form it persists 6 months or more and is relatively intractable to the traditional, biomedical treatment. It varies in severity, and may involve any of a number of muscle groups. Examples for such pain form are low back pain, myofascial pain syndrome, and tension headache. Chronic progressive pain persists much longer than 6 months and gradually increases in its severity and is typically associated with rheumatoid arthritis, degenerative disorders, obstructive pulmonary disease, and cancer (Taylor, 1995).

EPIDEMIOLOGY OF CHRONIC PAIN

Several epidemiological studies show a significant prevalence of pain experiences among the population. They point out the importance of appropriate therapeutic approach as also the problems of patient's adherence during the healing process.

A World Health Organisation (WHO) survey of primary care patients in 15 countries reported that *22 percent* of patients reported pain present for 6 months or longer that required medical attention, medication or interfered significantly with their daily activities (Gureje, 1998). In United Kingdom it was found that 25 percent of adult experienced back or neck pain in the prior month, with half reporting chronic pain (Webb et al., 2003). Sheffield (1998) estimated that migraine has a worldwide prevalence of approximately of 10 percent.

Turk and Melzack (2011) submitted the results of American National Centre of Health Statistics, NCHS (2006) that 1 of 4 adult Americans reported an episode of pain during the last month that persist more than 24 hours. It was also found that approximately *25 percent of US population* has chronic or recurrent pain (1 person of 10 reported a pain which lasted a year or more), and 40 percent of them stated the pain had a moderately or severely degrading impact on their lives. Authors also indicated data of National Health Interview Survey that during 3 months prior to the survey, 15 percent of adults had experienced a migraine or severe headache, 15 percent experienced neck pain, 27 percent had lower back pain, and 4 percent jaw. According to the National Headache Foundation (2005) more than 45 million American experience chronic headaches, with losses of 50 billion a year due to absenteeism and medical expenses, an excess of 4 billion spent on over- the counter medications.

As pain is very common symptom in healthcare some estimates that around *80 per cent* of people who see a doctor are in pain. (Skevington, 2004). Following to this, an experience of pain may be the primary reason that people seek medical care. Authors Stucky, Gold, and Zhang (2001) reported that over one-third of the world's population suffers from persistent or recurrent chronic pain, costing for example alone the American public approximately 100 billion dollars each year in health care, compensation, and litigation.

Introducing a brief review of occurrence of some non-malignant kinds of pain we first presented the research of von Kroff, Dworkin, LeResche, and Kruger (1988). They have found that *back pain prevalence* for a period of 6 months increases with the age in men (33 percent to 46 percent), unlike women who have shown the opposite trend (47 percent to 34 percent). But as the data on age and sex specific prevalence varied from study to study, no clear inferences can be drawn, except that back pain prevalence appears to rise in men up to age 50.

Stewart, Schechter, and Rasmussen (1994) found that one year *prevalence of migraine* for women ranged from 12, 9 to 17, 7 percent, and that by men ranged from 3, 4 to 6, 1 percent. In addition, other studies have shown also a higher prevalence of migraine in women of all ages. It has been found that gender ratio increase in women after the onset of menarche to 42 years and then falls, but remains about 2:1 in those over 60. The highest prevalence for both men and women has been found in period from 35 to 45 years.

Rasmussen et al., found that 1 year *prevalence of tension headache* decline with age in women and is highest in period of 25-34 year. For men rates were highest in the 45-54 year age group. In each age group the prevalence of tension headache was higher in women than for men. The vast majority of tension type of headache had episodic headache, whereas approximately 3 percent of the total population met criteria of chronic headache (headache 180 days per year or more).

Joint pain is associated with rheumatoid arthritis and osteoarthritis. As the overall prevalence of RA is estimated at about 1 percent (Mc Duffie,1985; Wolf, 1994) and presuming that almost all active cases of RA are associated with pain, it could be an accurate reflection of the with RA associated pain presence. Onset of RA is rare before age 40, but the prevalence of RA increased with age in both genders with overall prevalence in women about three times more than in men (Wolfe, 1994). OA changes are less associated with the onset of pain. However, research (Lawrence, Bremmer, and Bier, 1966) has shown that this type of pain increased with age in both genders, in women twice as much as in men of the same age (over age 65 prevalence in women is 31 percent, and in men 15 percent). Lawrence et al. (1966) emphasizes that the age specific prevalence of joint pain certainly reflects the degenerative changes which are expressed over the years, in women higher than in men (in Le Resche and Von Korff, 1999).

CHRONIC PAIN AND QUALITY OF LIFE

There is growing awareness among health care providers that quality of life is an important health outcome in assessing the functioning of the chronically ill, which is always their subjective experience that can be best rated by them. *Quality of live is usually defined as the individuals' perception of their functioning and well-being in different domains of the life* (Fayers and Machin, 2000) or in more specific terms, as the individuals' evaluation of their position in the life, in the context of culture and value system in which their live, and in the relation to their goals, expectations, standards and concerns (WHOQoL, 1995). Quality of life (QoL) is generally considered to have several components: *physical status and functioning, psychological status, social functioning, and disease or treatment related symptomatology* (Coons and Kaplan, 1992; in Taylor, 1995). Most tools for assessing QoL rely on the individuals' self-report and provide scores comparable across participants in the applied questionnaires (WHOQoL, S-36, PGWB, NHP, MSQoL; in Kreitler and Niv, 2007).

A great number of studies in different countries with hundreds of pain patients suffering from pain due to different causes and diagnoses show that the pain experience significant decrease individual's quality of life (Garrat, Ruta, Abdala et al., 1993; Becker, Thomsen, Olsen et al., 1997; Hagen, Kvien and Bjorndal, 1997; Skevington, 1998). It was found that QoL scores of pain patients could be even lower than those with gastrointestinal symptoms, hypertension, cardiopulmoraly disease or major depression (Stewart et al., 1988; Well, Stewart, Hays et al., 1989; Ware, Gandek, and IOQLA Project Group, 1994; Becker et al., 1997; Arnold, Witzeman, Swank et al., 2000).

It was also found that to the lowering the pain patient's QoL contribute pain characteristics as *pain intensity* (the more intense the pain, the lower is QoL, Rummans e al., 1998, Skevington, 1998), *extent of body area* (the QoL is lower when the area is extensive than when pain is regional - Croft, Rigby, Boswell et al., 1993; lower by two kind of pain than when exists only one kind of pain – Dartigues, Michel, and Lindoulsi et al., 1998), *co-morbidity* (the QoL is lower by more than one disease, even when the additional is not related to pain - Cuijpers, van Lammern, and Duzijn, 1999), *pain duration* (the QoL is lower when the pain lasts longer – Skevington, 1998), *and pain components* (the QoL is lower by emotional and evaluative components of pain but not by the sensory one – Passchier, de Boo, Quaark et al., 1996).

The impact of pain on QoL is also negative affected by some *demographic characteristics* as they are: lower education level, older age, being a female and unemployed. Age and gender played a role regard to the domain in which the deterioration has been shown, for example, in older male patients – prevailing are problems in physical function and vitality; in older females – the main problems are found in emotional relationship (Allison et al., 1998; Redigor, Barrio, de la Fuente et al., 1999; in Kreitler and Niv, 2007).

A closer analysis in this field shown that in general, the most strongly affected domain of QoL are *physical* (mobility, working capacity, activity of daily living, feelings of discomfort, low level of energy, fatigue, sexual inactivity, sleep disorders), *emotional* (fear and anxiety, anger, negative mood, depression), and *social and cognitive domain* (Stewart et al., 1988; in Kreitler and Niv, 2007).

In fact, chronic pain can entirely disrupt a person's life. Many of painful sensations stressed persons so much that they lose interest in professional activity, reduce their aspirations and efforts, giving up leisure activities, withdrawn from their friends and other social contacts in social isolation

(Fordyce, 1976; Clarc, 1977). It does not reduce only their *professional productivity and efficiency, recreational and social life,* but it often brings conflicts within their *partnerships and family* as a whole. Because of lower work-ability such patients often lose their jobs, or more frequently, they carry out less demanding work. Consequently, because of lower income they experience *a decline in living standards.* Often they lose *self-esteem* and have therefore difficulty to perform simple tasks of self-care (Kerns and Turk, 1984; Flor, Turk, and Scholz, 1987). Many chronic pain patients *lose interest to sexual contacts,* turn inward, and become self-absorbed. They may not only reduce physical activity, they often *avoid personal contacts*, remain to be closed in their own world, *avoid any changes,* crowds, loud noises, bright lights, and so on. (Phillips, 1983; Fordyce, 1988). Many chronic pain patients are *depressed*, a large number of them are considering or have already *attempted suicide* (in Taylor, 1995; Turk and Okifuji, 2002; Turk and Monarch, 2002).

CHRONIC PAIN AND COPING

In general coping is defined as ability to generate and maintain psychological well-being despite living with a serious condition (Folkman, 1997), and is linked to better psychological adjustment outcomes (Smith et al., 1997).

Self regulation of a pain and its effects depends on the person's specific ways of dealing with pain. It can be assessed in terms of *active*, such as information seeking and self-management, and *passive*, such as catastrophizing and wishful thinking, as also in terms of *overt* (rest, medication, relaxation) and *covert* (distracting oneself from pain, reassuming oneself pain will diminish) *behaviour patterns*. The coping strategies, of this or that type, could act to alter both the perception of a pain and the one's ability to manage or tolerate a pain and to continue the everyday activities (Turk and Okifuji, 2002).

A number of studies have demonstrated that if people are instructed in the use of *adaptive coping strategies* (problem focused coping, regular exercise, positive self-statements, social comparison) their ratings of pain intensity decrease and tolerance for pain increases (Fernandez and Turk, 1989). This may be a good reason to know more about the pain related coping style and strategies.

Researches on coping with pain identified several coping strategies related to the adjustment to pain and usually used one or more of following outcome measures to assess the adjustment: higher level of psychological distress, more negative affects and less positive affects, less uptime, higher rates of analgesic use, more pain-related physician visits, more frequent and longer hospitalizations, more reports of pain, higher ratings of pain intensity, lower level of general activity, more psychosocial dysfunctions, reduced ability to work, lower rate of return to work. Review of studies up to 1991 as well as later showed that passive coping strategies such as wishful thinking, praying, restricting activities, taking medication, calling a doctor are associated with increased pain, depression, distress, lower positive affects, disability and poorer psychological adjustment (Jensen, Turner, Romano, and Karoly, 1991; Zaura, Burleson, Smith et al., 1995; in Kreitler and Niv, 2007).

Most notable are the consistent findings about maladaptive function of the strategies of catastrophizing, hoping/praying, wishful thinking, pain contingent rest, guarding, avoidance of activities, using sedative-hypnotic medication, seeking of social support, comforting thinking, and palliative coping. Among them the *catastrophizing* ("I expect the worst", This pain will never get any better." "There is nothing I can do to relive my pain.") *is the most important factor in poor coping with pain.* Such extremely negative thoughts appear to be a particularly potent way of thinking that influences pain and disability and great number of surveys demonstrated its maladaptive nature in regard to different categories of pain patients. (Hill, 1993; Geisser, Keefe et al., 1994; Robinson et al., 1997). Particularly in clinical practice it could show its problematic effects when the pain complaints is of high intensity but poorly localized (Hadjitavropoulos and Craig, 1994; in Kreitler and Niv, 2007). Main and Wadell (1991) as also Wells (1994) found that people who spontaneously use more catastrophizing self-statements reported more pain, distress, and disability in several acute and chronic pain studies. And conversely, people who use fewer catastrophizing self-statements and more adaptive coping strategies rated the induced pain as lower and they also tolerated painful stimuli longer (Spanos, Horton and Chaves, 1975; Heyneman, Fremouw, Gano, Kirkland and Heiden, 1990; in Turk and Monarch, 2002).

From my own research (Rakovec-Felser, 1997), which included an accidental group of patients with tension type headaches and separately, an equivalent group of people with lower back pain, it is evident that they both, in comparison with the group without health problems, show significantly less constructive coping strategies. Instead of being focused on solving problems, in everyday life they tend to adopt short-term solutions, as they offer some kind of emotional release or substitute feelings of comfort. They negate or minimize problems and find reasons for them in unfavourable external conditions. They show fatalism ("I gave up, this is my fate, I am usually unlucky.") and instead of enduring effort they choose momentary comfort. Rather than active resolve, they prefer imaginary achievements. In social relations they are active and able to seek help, but in contact with others they favour emotional support much more than information and orientation in problem solving. In the context of the other instruments employed in the study, their coping style is seen primarily as part of their personality rather than merely a result of pain experience and the described poor mood.

However, passive strategies, although generally non-productive in altering both the perception of the pain and one's quality of life, can sometimes be productive. In other words, the effectiveness of active coping strategies may also vary, depending on the characteristics of pain intensity and pain duration. For example, avoidance coping, which considered in general as a negative strategy could be useful in the initial stages of pain, but when this unpleasant sensation persist, such strategy could increasingly lead to maladjustment (Kreitler and Niv, 2007). This was well expressed by Turk and Okifuji (2002), who state that different coping strategies could be more effective than others for some people at some times, but not necessary for all people all of the time.

CHRONIC PAIN FROM COGNITIVE-BEHAVIOURAL PERSPECTIVE

Health behaviour reveals how people perceive, understand, and manage their health troubles. Understanding the factors affecting the patient's health behaviour is the best way to reduce the number of disagreements between patients and physicians. This consequently leads to a higher level of patient adherence, and therefore to more effective health care.

There are several theoretical models which were developed to predict and explain health behaviour. The highly influential and widely researched theory of why people practice health behaviours is *Health Belief Model* (Hochbaum, 1958; Rosenstock, 1966). From this perspective, health behaviour can be understood as the person's response to how seriously he/she perceives a health threat and how effectively he/she perceives health practice in reducing that threat. The perception of a personal health threat is influenced by general health values, interests and concern about health, specific beliefs about vulnerability to a particular disorder, beliefs about the consequences of disorder, and taking or not taking medications (Taylor, 1995).

Following this, many researchers attempted to identify the cognitive-behaviour patterns contributing to pain and disability (Jensen, Turner, Romano, and Karoly, 1991; Turk and Rudy, 1992; DeGood and Tait, 2001). It was found that patients' attitudes, beliefs, and expectancies (to their plight, themselves, coping resources, and to health care system), affected their reports of pain, activity, disability, as also response to a treatment (Flor and Turk, 1988; Tota-Faucette, Gil, Williams, and Goli, 1993; Jensen, Turner, Romano, and Lawler, 1994). People who believe that their pain is likely to persist may be quite passive in their coping efforts and may fail to make use of cognitive or behavioural strategies to cope with pain. Pain sufferers who consider their pain to be an unexplainable mystery may minimize their own abilities to control or decrease pain and may be less likely to rate their coping strategies as effective in controlling and decreasing pain (Williams and Thorn, 1989; Williams and Keefe, 1991). A person's cognitions (*beliefs, appraisals, expectancies*) regarding the consequences of an event and his or her ability to deal with it are hypothesized to affect functioning in two ways—by directly influencing mood and indirectly influencing coping efforts. Both influences may affect physiological activity associated with pain such as *muscle tension* (Flor et al., 1985) and production of *endogenous opioids* (Bandura et al., 1987).

The presence of pain may change the way people process pain-related and other information. For example, chronic pain may focus attention on all types of bodily signals. Arntz and Schmidt (1989) have suggested that in the chronic pain patients a processing of internal information may become disturbed. It is possible because pain patients may be preoccupied with physical symptoms. In such a mental state they could perceive even less disruptive stimuli as more unfavourable and as painful stimulation. It is also known that patients who believed that they were disabled by pain and should avoid activity because pain signified damage were more likely to reveal physical disability than were patients who did not hold these beliefs. Once cognitive structures, based on memories and meaning about a disease are formed, they become stable and difficult to modify. Patients tend to avoid experiences that could invalidate their beliefs, and they guide their behaviour in accordance with these beliefs even in situations in which the beliefs are no longer valid. The results of several studies suggest that it is only in the case of an effective rehabilitation observed significant cognitive shift - a shift from beliefs about helplessness and passivity to resourcefulness and ability to function regardless of pain.

Similarly, Williams and Thorn (1989) found that chronic pain patients who believed that their pain was an "unexplained mystery" reported high levels of psychological distress and pain and also showed poorer treatment compliance than did patients who believed that they understood their pain.

Many studies results demonstrate that *controllability* of aversive stimulation reduces its negative impact (Jensen and Karoly, 1991; Wells, 1994). Conversely, there is evidence that the explicit expectation of uncontrollable pain stimulation may cause subsequent nociceptive pain input to be perceived as more intense (Leventhal and Everhart, 1979). Because people who have associated activity with pain may expect heightened levels of pain when they attempt to get involved in activity, they may actually perceive higher levels of pain or avoid activity altogether. Chronic pain sufferers typically perceive a lack of personal control, which probably relates to their ongoing but unsuccessful efforts to influence the pain they experience. A large proportion of chronic pain patients appear to believe that they have limited ability to exert control over their pain (Turk and Rudy, 1988). Such negative, maladaptive appraisals about the situation and their personal efficacy may reinforce the experience of demoralization, inactivity, and overreaction to nociceptive stimulation (Biedermann, McGhie, Monga, and Shanks, 1987).

Closely related to the need for control is the *concept* of *Self-efficacy*. A self-efficacy expectation is defined as a personal conviction that one can successfully execute a course of action (perform required behaviours) to produce a desired outcome in a given situation. This construct appears to be a major mediator of therapeutic change. Bandura (1986, 1994, 1997) suggested that self-efficacy determine the goals people set for themselves, how much effort they expend, how long they persevere in the face of obstacles and aversive experiences. People with high assurance in their capabilities approach difficult tasks as challenges to be mastered rather than as treats to be avoided. Such an efficacious outlook fosters intrinsic interest and commitment to action. Strong perseverance contributes to performance accomplishments and finally, to higher *perceived coping self-efficacy*. People's beliefs in their coping capabilities affect how much stress and depression they experience in threatening situation, as well as their level of motivation. Perceived self-efficacy to exercise control over stressors plays a central role in anxiety arousal. People who believe they can exercise control over threats do not conjure up disturbing thought patterns. But those who believe they cannot manage threats experience much more anxiety and view many aspects of their environment as dangerous. They attach greater weight to the possible barriers, and are worried about things that have not yet occurred. On account of such inefficient thinking, they distress themselves and are less effective in daily functioning. It follows that anxiety arousal is affected not only by perceived coping efficacy but also by *perceived efficacy to control disturbing thoughts*. The exercise of control over one's own consciousness is summed up well in the proverb: "You cannot prevent the birds of worry and care from flying over your head. But you can stop them from building a nest in your head." Therefore are both perceived coping self-efficacy and thought control efficacy responsible and operate jointly to reduce or increase an anxiety and avoidant behaviour.

CHRONIC PAIN AND EMOTIONAL RESPONSES

In order to understand the reasons for low or non-adherence of the chronic pain patient, it is not enough to know the level of their quality of life and efficacy of their coping efforts. It is important to also take into account their health beliefs, expectations and values, as well as the emotional responses to the pain which they experience.

The affective components of pain include many different emotions, but they are primarily negative in quality. Romano and Turner (1985) concluded that 40 to 50 percent of chronic pain patients suffer from *depression*. In the majority of cases, depression appears to be patients' reaction to their plight. But why all people with chronic pain are not depressed? Turk and colleagues (Rudy, Kerns, and Turk, 1988; Turk et al., 1994, 1995; Okifuji, Turk, and Sherman, 2000) examined this question and determined that patients' appraisals of the impact of the pain on their lives and of their ability to exert any control over their pain and lives mediated the pain–depression relationship. Patients, who believed that they could continue to function despite their pain, and maintain some control despite their pain, did not become depressed.

Feelings of *fear, tension, restlessness, and worry* are common companions of pain, especially chronic (Vlaeyen, Kole-Snijders, Boeren, and van Eek, 1995). *Anxiety* is an affective state that is influenced by appraisal processes. There is a reciprocal relationship between affective state and cognitive–interpretive processes whereby thinking affects mood and mood influences appraisals and ultimately the experience of pain. Fear of pain and anticipation of pain are cognitive–perceptual processes that are not driven exclusively by the actual sensory experience of pain and can exert a significant impact on the level of function and pain tolerance (Feuerstein and Beattie, 1995; Vlaeyen et al., 1999).

Fear of pain, driven by the anticipation of pain and not by sensory experience of pain, is a strong negative reinforcement for the persistence of avoidance behaviour and functional disability (Lenthem et al., 1983; Vlaeyen, Kole-Snijders, Rooteveel, Ruesink, and Heuts, 1995). Avoidance can be a maladaptive response if it persists and leads to increased fear, limited activity, and other physical and psychological consequences that contribute to disability and persistence of pain. Studies have demonstrated that fear of movement and fears of (re)injury are better predictors of functional limitations than are biomedical parameters - for example, laboratory data, EMG, CT, MRI (McCracken et al., 1993; Vlaeyen, Kole-Snijders, Rooteveel, et al., 1995).

Another pain associated emotion is *anger*. It has been widely observed in patients with chronic pain (see, e.g., Fernandez and Turk, 1995; Schwartz, Slater, Birchler, and Atkinson, 1991). Summers, Rapoff, Varghese, Porter, and Palmer (1992) examined patients with spinal cord injuries and found that anger and hostility explained 33 percent of the variance in pain severity. Kerns, Rosenberg, and Jacobs (1994) found that the internalization of angry feelings accounted for a significant proportion of variances in measures of pain intensity, perceived interference, and reported frequency of pain behaviours. Frustrations related to persistence of symptoms, limited information on aetiology, and repeated treatment failures, along with anger toward employers, insurance companies, health care system, family members, and themselves, all these contributes to the general dysphoric mood of patients (Okifuji, Turk, and Curran, 1999). Anger may also block motivation for and acceptance of treatments oriented toward rehabilitation and disability management rather than cure. It is important to be aware of the role of negative mood in pain sufferers because it is likely to affect treatment motivation and compliance with treatment recommendations. For example, patients who are depressed and who feel helpless may have little initiative to comply, patients who are anxious may fear engaging in what they perceive as physically demanding activities, and patients who are angry at the health care system are not likely to be motivated to respond to recommendations from yet another health care professional. Therefore it is reasonable to suggest that anger serves as a complicating factor. (Fernandez and Turk, 1995).

In our study (Rakovec-Felser, 1997) of chronic pain patients we found signs of anxiety, suppressed aggression, and depression, but also the other specifics of their emotional responses have been identified. By using Strelau Temperament Inventory (STI, Strelau, 1970-1999) which based on theory of strength of excitation, inhibition, and mobility of nervous processes, we found that patients with pain (tension headache and low back pain) are more susceptible to external stimuli, they previously experienced a neutral stimuli as disruptive, and are therefore also faster and harder aroused than persons without health problems.

As a result, they previously consumed their adaptive potential, are faster exhausted and without energy. In the state of exhaustion their threshold for pain decreases. Except of a higher degree of irritability and lower tolerance to daily pressure, they also show a reduce control over their impulses, and they slowly return from the state of arousal and excitation to the state of internal balance.

ADHERENCE IN THE BIOMEDICAL MANAGEMENT OF CHRONIC PAIN

Traditional approach to management of chronic pain is usually combination of pharmacological and physical therapies, in the case of back pain the surgical interventions seems to be considered as gold standard for its treatment. Generally, according to researchers in this field the rates of pain reduction ranged from 0 (Sturgis, Schaefer, and Sicora, 1984; Deardorff, Rubin and Scott, 1991) to 60 percent (Moore, Berk, and Nypaver, 1984; Tollison, Kriegel, and Downie, 1985).

Adherence to a medication regimen is generally defined as the extent to which patients take medications as were prescribed by their health care providers. Rates of adherence for individual patients are usually reported as the percentage of the prescribed doses of the medication actually taken by the patient over a specified period (rates of 80 percent or higher). Adherence rates are typically higher among patients with acute conditions, as compared with those with chronic conditions; adherence can vary along a continuum from 0 to more than 100 percent (Osterberg and Blaschke, 2005). Signs of low or non-adherence (at 40 to 75 percent of patients, average at 50 percent) may be:

- Choose not to take their medication regularly due to fear of addiction,
- Take too little medication, or none at all, because of the costs or side effects,
- Take too much medication because of inadequate pain control or addiction,

- Divert their pain medications – whether unintentionally or intentionally;

In relation to other chronic conditions adherence in patients with chronic, especially non-malignant pain, may be substantial differences. The chronic non-malignant (or benign) pain is defined by the International Association for the Study of Pain (IASP) as pain that persists beyond the normal time of healing. It is so called due to non-life-threatening causes (e.g., tension headache, migraine, back pain, neuropathic pain, etc.), has not responded to currently available treatment methods, and may continue for the remainder of the person's life (Wall and Melzack, 1999). According to the World Health Organization (WHO, 2003), chronic non-malignant pain can be considered as a chronic disease that typically includes one or more of the following characteristics: it is permanent, leaves residual disability, is caused by non-reversible pathological alterations, requires special training for rehabilitation, or may be expected to require a long period of supervision, observation, or care (Sabaté, 2003, WHO).

The prevalence of chronic pain is relatively high, affecting about *19 percent* of the general population in Europe, North America, and Australia. (Verhaak, Kerssens, Dekker, Sorbi, and Bensing, 1998; Blyth, March, Brnabic, Jorm, Williamson, and Cousins, 2001; Breivik, Collett, Ventafridda, Cohen, and Gallacher, 2006). The most frequently chronic pain disorder is chronic back pain, affecting about half of the chronic pain sufferers (Breivik, Collett, Ventafridda, Cohen, and Gallacher, 2006). Other common pain conditions are headache, neuropathic pain, chronic widespread pain, and fibromyalgia. The pathophysiology of chronic benign pain is not entirely clear, but involves complex interactions between physical, psychological, and social issues (Wall and Melzack, 1999).

Due to the complex nature of chronic pain, its treatment demands an individualized approach, preferably provided by a specialized multidisciplinary pain team. Although adequate treatment focuses on several aspects, such as physical rehabilitation and psychological strategies to cope with chronic pain, the medication, however, often remains a cornerstone of chronic pain treatment.

Epidemiological studies in a general population show that in more than 50 percent of the chronic pain sufferers, medication is part of their pain treatment (Andersson, Ejlertsson, Leden, and Schersten, 1999; Catala, Reig, Artes, Aliaga, Lopez, and Segu, 2002; Vallerand, Fouladbakhsh, and Templin, 2005; Breivik, Collett, Ventafridda, Cohen, and Gallacher, 2006). In pain centres, this percentage is even higher, amounting to over 80 percent of the included patients (Ready, Sarkis, and Turner, 1982; Berndt, Maier, and Schutz, 1993; Kouyanou, Pither, and Wessely, 1997). Besides pain reduction the improved sleep, daily activities and mood should be important treatment endpoints for patients as well (Casarett, Karlawish, Sankar, Hirschman, and Asch, 2001).

As chronic non-malignant pain often not responds to the available biomedical treatment options and could continues for the remainder of a person's life, *this population of patients is highly susceptible for dissatisfaction with care* (Hirsh, Atchison, Berger, Waxenberg, Lafayette-Lucey, and Bulcourf, 2005). It was found that level of satisfaction with chronic pain treatment related to several factors, such as patients *mental health, their kind of coping strategies and the patient-physician relation* (Hirsh, Atchison, Berger, Waxenberg, Lafayette-Lucey, and Bulcourf, 2005; McCracken, Klock, Mingay, Asbury, and Sinclair, 1997; Brekke, Hjortdahl, and Kvien, 2001; McCracken, Evon, and Karapas, 2002; in Turk and Monarch 2002).

Broekmans (2011) who analyzed the results of some research conclude that low or non adherence with prescribed pain medication taking (analgesics, anxiolytics, antidepressants) is a major problem in patients with chronic non-malignant pain. The prevalence of medication non-adherence ranges from *7,7 to 52,9 percent*. The studies suggest, she notes, that medication underuse is more common than medication overuse. Such, the underuse form of non-adherence in chronic benign pain patients seem to be at least as likely compared to other chronic disease populations because chronic non-malignant pain is a chronic, but not a life-threatening condition. Patients believe that abandonment of pills will not have such negative effects on their health status as in other cases. A meta-analysis across 27 studies medical conditions showed a strongly positive relationship between respondents' adherence and their perception of disease severity (DiMatteo, Haskard, and Williams, 2007), as also that the patients' beliefs about their medicines could predicted adherence (Horne and Weinman, 1999; Mardby, Akerlind, and Jorgensen, 2007) Beliefs about the necessity of prescribed medication for maintaining health or avoiding illness are weighed against concerns about negative effects of taking it (Horne and Weinman, 1999). McCracken, Hoskins, and Eccleston (2006) found that underuse of medication is predicted by concern over side-effects and relatively little perceived need or concern about withdrawal. They also found that overuse is predominantly predicted by perceiving medication as needed and secondarily related to concern about negative scrutiny (Broekmans, 2011).

Graziottin et al. (2011) cite the WHO data, that adherence factors are related to *the patient, condition, therapy, health-care team and system,* as also *to the social and economic factors* (Sabaté, WHO, 2003). Positive influences for improving adherence include a basic knowledge of the disease, good motivation with respect to treatment, the patient's faith in his or her ability to self-manage the therapeutic regimen, and finally, solid expectations in terms of treatment efficacy (Sabaté, WHO, 2003; Graziottin, 2007; Berliner, Stumpf, and, Bornhövd, 2008).

On the other side depression may be one of the most powerful factors for non-adherence to therapy and interruption of treatment (Graziottin, 2007). Other negative factors reducing adherence include lack of faith in the doctor and/or health service, anxiety, high levels of emotional and psychosocial stress, financial problems, and fear of adverse events, cultural or religious beliefs, and failure to perceive a personal benefit or greater physical or psychological well-being in comparison with not taking medicine. Previous research in chronic pain patients already showed that patients who said they were not well informed by the physician were more likely to underuse their medication (Broekmans, Dobbels, Milisen, Morlion, and Vanderschueren, 2010). Numerous studies and meta-analyses have shown that *the more complex the treatment regimen, the worse is the adherence* (Stone, 1979; Mulleners et al., 1998; Winkler, 2002; Kardas, 2005; Portsmouth, 2005). Graziottin et al. (2007) advises next measures to improve the adherence to doctor's recommendations:

- A patient-doctor relationship and the treatment strategies should based on the patient's choices, allowing the patient to participate in the therapeutic decisions;
- An empathic attitude towards the intrusiveness of the pain and its meaning in the patient's life is way in improving the dialogue and ensuring that the patient feels fully understood and supported;
- Defined treatment objectives (the doctor and patient should discuss the achievable objectives and the time needed to achieve them);
- Tools for disease prognosis (tools involving prognosis, can facilitate the decision to initiate, or withdraw, long-term treatment with analgesics);
- Simple treatment regimens (treatment regimens that have a low dosing frequency of medication and fit into the daily routine should be used);

- Identification of patients at higher risk of side effects or drug abuse (detailed questioning on predisposing, precipitating, or maintaining factors for severe constipation and/or for drug abuse should be routinely included in the history taking and decision making process);
- Management of side effects (possible side effects should be fully explained to the patient and treated pro-actively);
- Monitoring treatment success (satisfaction with analgesics is associated with the perception of a specific improvement, i.e., a reduction in pain or an increase in well-being; increased perception of satisfaction of use may motivate the patient to continue therapy);
- Anti-depressant management (depression should be carefully monitored and treated appropriately);
- Support within the community (Family members or friends can remind the patient to take their medication and/or assist with preparing dosage receptacles to enhance compliance);
- Educational program for patients and carers (Improving the understanding of the benefits and side-effects of the treatment regimen may help to motivate patients to follow the therapy correctly. Educating relatives and/or caregivers in understanding chronic pain and being positive and proactive about analgesics and other pain management medication and strategies will increase the overall adherence to achieve effective pain control (Graziottin, Gardner-Nix, Stumpf, and Berliner, 2011).

People with chronic pain over time show some form of emotional disturbance, cognitive difficulties, inability to work and fatigue. Therefore, medical treatment, focusing on pain relief alone, will be insufficient to treat the complex problem of chronic pain. Current treatment approaches for chronic pain should cover physical, psychological, and environmental factors and involve a multidisciplinary pain management approach (Turk, 2002). Therefore, in this case it might be more important to focus on interventions, which will improve patients' satisfaction, instead of pursuing strict adherence, emphasizes the author. So improving communication between patient and healthcare provider might be a successful strategy, consider also other researchers (Zolnierek and DiMatteo 2009). Patients need to know the benefits and side-effects of medication and physicians need to know patients' beliefs and attitudes towards medicine taking. Educating patients about their medication and potential side effects can empower them to alter their perceptions and to participate actively in decisions about medication taking, in

1995 sees the solution Edwards (Broekmans, Dobbels, Milisen, Morlion, Vanderschueren, 2010). Butow says (2012) that patients with pain don't like taking pills, because they worry about side effects and about addiction to pain medication. Patients could also worry that admitting pain reflects their weak character. She sees the solution in doctor-patient communication as a way to encourage patients to talk about their pain, reassure them, to address misconceptions and barriers and to identify what is most important to them in managing their pain and tailoring pain medication (Butow, 2012).

In prescribed exercise the participation is even more dependent on individual's motives. They are related to type, extent, and stage of exercise participation. In field of physiotherapy, the concept of adherence is multi-dimensional (Kolt et al., 2007) and could relate to attendance at appointments, following advice, undertaking prescribed exercises, frequency of undertaking prescribed exercise, correct performance of exercises or doing more or less than advised. Many factors related to the patient, the healthcare provider and the healthcare organisation are thought to influence patient adherence with treatment (Miller et al., 1997).

Identification of barriers may help clinicians identify patients at risk of non-adherence and suggest methods to reduce the impact of those barriers thereby maximising adherence. Group of researchers Jack, Mc Lean, Moffett, and Gardiner (2010) systematic review the results from 20 high quality studies and found strong evidence that low levels of physical activity at baseline or in previous weeks, low in-treatment adherence with exercise, low self-efficacy, depression, anxiety, helplessness, poor social support or activity, greater perceived number of barriers to exercise and increased pain levels during exercise are barriers to treatment adherence.

They mean that physiotherapists need to recognise reasons and be ready to mitigate the barriers to adherence in exercise programmes. Reasons for low adherence can be found in poor programme organisation and leadership, poor education, poor history of exercise, perceived physical weakness, perceived poor health, and unwillingness to change (Duncan and McAuley, 1993; Courneya and McAuley, 1995; Boyette et al., 1997; Hellman, 1997; Rhodes et al., 1999). Practical barriers may be transportation problems, child care needs, work schedules, lack of time, family dependents, financial constraints, convenience, and forgetting. It is right that physiotherapists are aware of difficulties that patients foresee in relation to adhering with a proposed treatment plan and that they act collaboratively with their patients to design treatment plans which are customised to the patient's life circumstances (Turk and Rudy, 1991).

Common barriers to treatment adherence are also depression (Minor and Brown, 1993; Shaw et al., 1994; Rejeski et al., 1997; Oliver and Cronan, 2002), anxiety (Minor and Brown, 1993; Dobkin et al., 2006), and helplessness (Sluijs et al., 1993; Castenada et al., 1998). Simultaneously ensuring that pain is being effectively managed with physiotherapeutic measures may be helpful in reducing anxiety or depression which is pain related. Additionally it may be helpful to reinforce the message that exercise is an effective way of countering both low mood and negative thoughts, whilst simultaneously improving pain and function (Lim et al., 2005). Greater social support and encouragement for exercise in this group of patients may provide motivation, role models, and guidance (Castenada et al., 1998).

Low self-efficacy was also identified as a barrier to treatment adherence (Shaw et al., 1994; Taylor and May, 1996; Stenstrom et al., 1997; Chen et al., 1999; Oliver and Cronan, 2002; Milne et al., 2005). Poor self-efficacy could explain a patient's low confidence in their ability to overcome obstacles to initiating, maintaining, or recovering from relapses in exercise (Sniehotta et al., 2005). Low self-efficacy could be identified by clinicians using simple questions such as "How confident are you that you can…" (a)…"overcome obstacles to exercising?" or (b)…"return to exercise, despite having relapsed for several weeks?" Strategies to address low self-efficacy should be specific to the individual's stage of exercise behaviour or perceived obstacles (Scholz et al., 2005). The use of strategies such as agreeing realistic expectations (Jensen and Lorish, 1994), setting treatment goals (Evans and Hardy, 2002), action planning (Sniehotta et al., 2005), coping planning and positive reinforcement (Gohner and Schlicht, 2006) may help increase patient self-efficacy and adherence.

Group of researchers (Funch and Gale, 1986; Minor and Brown, 1993; Sluijs et al., 1993; Rejeski et al., 1997; Oliver and Cronan, 2002) found that low levels of social activity and low social or family support (Shaw et al., 1994) are also the barriers to treatment adherence. Some patients believe that they would be more readily to exercise if they are accompanied by someone from relatives or other nearly persons (Milroy and O'Neil, 2000; Campbell et al., 2001). The support provided by the physiotherapists, their positive feedback may also increase patient's treatment adherence (Sluijs et al., 1993; Campbell et al., 2001). They could consider about rehabilitation programmes which incorporate social contact and support and in this way stimulate the patient's adherence.

Whereas participation motives are contents of goals for participating, behavioural regulations represent the perceived locus of causality of the goal.

This conception of behavioural regulations has been developed within the framework of Self-determination theory of Deci and Ryan (2000): people are intrinsically motivated when they engage in an activity for the inherent satisfaction that they derive from the activity ("I exercise because it is fun") in contrast to extrinsically motivated when they engage in an activity for the separable outcomes that they attain though the activity whether rewards attained or punishments avoided ("I exercise because others say I should"). External and introjected regulation is classed as controlled motivation. Identified, integrated and intrinsic regulation is classed as autonomous motivation. Generally, more autonomous motivation is associated with sustained engagement in the behaviour. This has been found for various health promoting behaviours (Williams, 2002), including exercise participation (Mullan and Markland, 1997; Wilson, Rodgers and Fraser, 2002; Wilson, Rodgers, Blanchard and Gesell, 2003; Landry and Solmon, 2004; in Ingledew, Markland, 2008).

The surgical literature indicates that approximately *57 to 70 percent of patients* who have undergone *lumbar surgeries* continue to report significant levels of pain following treatment (Dvorak, Gauchat, and Valach, 1988; North et al. 1991; Wilkinson, 1993). It is estimated that the chronic pain patients have an average of 1,7 surgeries prior to being included in the multidisciplinary treatment (Flor et al., 1992). In the group of *conventional treated chronic pain patients* they are *28 to 47 percent* of such in which the additional hospitalization and surgery are needed (Cassisi, Sypert, Salamon, and Kapel, 1989; Tollison, Kriegel, Satterthwaite, and Turner, 1989; Tollison, 1991). But also serious complications following surgery that require additional surgery are relatively common. Long et al., (1988) reported that up to *35 percent of repeat back surgeries* were performed to treat problems associated with previous surgeries (Okifuji, Turk, and Kalauokalani, 1999).

ADHERENCE IN BIOPSYCHOSOCIAL APPROACH TO CHRONIC PAIN

The optimal management of most chronic illnesses requires a complex array of behaviour responsibilities, including lifestyle changes, use of medication, monitoring the symptoms or signs of illnesses. Adherence to so much complex behaviour regimens is influences by numerous variables. In the case of chronic pain, which is complex, multi-factorial phenomenon involving *sensory, cognitive, affective and behavioural* components that affect not only patient's well being, but it also leads to undesired changes in family relationships, as well as to social and occupational changes, the management of chronic pain should be therefore *multidimensional, multidisciplinary, multimodal nature* (Cohen and Campbell, 1996; in Kerns, Bayer, and Findley, 1999). It is understandable that in such a complex therapeutically approach, which typically includes tree common elements - *medication management, graded physical exercise, and cognitive-behavioural management* - the issue of adherence is complex.

In general, the treatment adherence can be define as the extent to which a person's behaviour coincides with treatment recommendation, or special in the case of non-malignant chronic pain as the extent of self-motivated decisions and willingness to self regulating of pain suffering and its treatment. The extent of adherence is related with two phenomena, namely, noncompliance with therapeutic recommendations during treatment and subsequent relapse after the treatment termination. Several factors that contribute to noncompliance (individual differences, nature of disease or injury, characteristics of the treatment regimen, health-care provider-patient relationship, and contextual) could lead also to relapse. Studies on heterogeneous pain clinic populations, namely, suggest that noncompliance and relapse are related (except in case of headache patients where this association is less well established). Claxton, Cramer, J. and Pierce (2001) reviewed 76 studies with an aggregated adherence rate of 71 percent, ranging from 34 percent to 97 percent across illnesses. Broekmans (2011) who analyzed the results of 27 researchers conclude that prevalence of medication non-adherence in patients with chronic non-malignant pain ranges from 7,7 to 52,9 percent. In the study Broekmans et al. (2010) it was found that 48 percent of the patients were non-adherent (34 percent with underuse and 14 percent overuse of the prescribed medication). The incidence of relapse following initially successful treatment of persistent pain also appears to be high, ranging from 30 to 60 per cent (Turk and Rudy, 1991).

How to recognize non-adherence in non-pharmacological treatment?

The examples of signs of non-adherence in this case could be the delays of seeking medical care, failure to keep treatment recommendations, advice, and appointments, failure to carry out a therapeutic homework, constant delays or/and absenteeism at therapeutically sessions, etc. In contrast to compliance the term adherence suggests more active patient role: a willingness to participate. Adherence also implies consistency with a therapeutic process; it is analogous to joining or attaching oneself to something, while compliance characterizes the patient as acquiescing, resigning, or relinquishing authority to another (Corrado, Griswold, and Murray, 2012).

In following we will focus on the problems of the pain patient's readiness to be an active participant in the psychological treatment. As part of a holistic approach, this treatment should be based on an integrative, primarily cognitive-behavioural therapy model with these phases:

- Initial assessment,
- Collaborative re-conceptualization of the patient's view of pain,
- Skills acquisition and skills consolidation, including cognitive and behavioural rehearsal,
- Generalization, maintenance, and relapse prevention,
- Booster sessions and follow up (Turk, 2002; Turk and Okifuji, 2003);

The long period of unsuccessful therapeutic attempts to stop their suffering (pharmacotherapy, anaesthetic treatments, surgery, physical therapy) and, consequently, their lost hope and confidence, mean that the chronic pain patient might have become embedded in a passive, "sick" role. Therefore, one of the therapeutic goals we must reach is moving towards interventions emphasizing a proactive and self-management approach. Psychological treatment should help patients conquer feelings of helplessness and hopelessness and from the very beginning it must be focused on the issues of patient motivation. Only a collaborative relationship between the patient and therapist can result in an effective course of treatment. The possibility to express their feelings about their pain and inefficient past treatment- related experience brings the patient an opportunity to release some tension, begin to acquire a better insight into their own position, and gradually to begin to trust in the therapist and therapeutic process (Rakovec-Felser, 1997).

Many such pain patients are overmedicated and on any way dependent on analgesics, sedatives, local anaesthetics drugs, antidepressants or sleeping pills and it will be advantageous to help them to reduce and eventually also to eliminate all unnecessary medication. If patient does not follow the doctor's guidelines in reducing of dosage, it should become a focus of opened discussion in psychological treatment because the attempt to control the medication intake is the first test of willingness to abandon inappropriate old patterns and to learn and adopt new views and behaviours (Turk and Okifuji, 2003). In this context, it was found that excessive analgesic or abortive medication use can both aggravate headache problems and limit benefits obtained to drug and nondrug therapies. Michultka et al. (1989) realized that persons with headache and high medications use significantly less than these with headache and low user benefit from both relaxation/thermal biofeedback training and psychological treatment. Low adherence and effects of treatment could be expected also by patients with concurrent psychiatric disorders and those who reported a history of parental alcoholism, sexual or physical abuse (Holroyd and French, 1995).

Successful initiation and engagement in treatment is crucial, particularly in light of report that initial level of treatment is the best predictor of long-term adherence (Sherbourne, Hays, Ordway, DiMatteo, and Krawitz, 1992; Berndt, Maier, and Schulz, 1993). But just this initial part of the treatment may be especially difficult. Some of this patients frame their pain in traditional model. Therefore they search for biomedical explanation and treatment of pain, but this could be completely inconsistent with the self-management of chronic pain and consequent altered quality of life.

Adoption of psychologically based interventions and self-management techniques may also threaten patients, implying that they are weak, histrionic, or malingering, or that others do not believe their pain is real (Schulz and Masek, 1996). Another barrier is issues of patients' adopted disability identity, their secondary gain. Particularly the patients who are seeking compensation through litigation may be in the treatment ambivalent. (DeGood and Dane, 1996). A new reason to resistance often appears when patients feel that their freedom being taken away or when they have sense that their ready to change being misunderstood. Choosing to talk about behaviour changes should be ultimately patient's choice. Given the role that readiness play in motivation to change behaviour, it can be useful to gain understanding of it. It is also necessary exploring how patient feel about changes. Achieving small changes can increase self-efficacy and make patients feel more able to make other small changes (Bandura, 1995). It is true that for changes patients need to be ready, willing, and able to make such step (Miller and Rollnick, 2002, in Kerns, Bayer, and Findley, 1999).

Therefore, it is important to start at a point where patients feel most comfortable and then encourage them to suggest which area they would choose ("There are a number of different things we can talk about today. I am just wondering what aspect of your lifestyle you would like to talk about."). Information during treatment is exchanged rather than simply provided to patients. Exchanging information and using the principles of Motivational Interviewing (MI) can encourage patients to actively think of how information given applies to themselves as individuals and can even save the therapist's time (Lane and Rollnick, 2009). As the interventions for chronic pain require patients to learn and implement a set of pain related coping and self-management skills, and acquisition of them involves making numerous behaviour changes, their motivation and readiness to enter into, continue, and adhere to specific change strategy play a key role in effective therapeutic approach. Responsibility for making changes also lies with patients, but therapist's behaviours play an integral role in developing and maintaining their motivation. Five principles of Motivational Interviewing could be helpful guidelines:

- Expressing empathy involves respect, acceptance of the patient by seeking to understand the patient's perspective and reflecting this as nonjudgmental stance back to the patient;
- Instead of confronting the patient, the therapist raises the patient's awareness of discrepancies between patient's current behaviours and his or her important life goals by listening for statements that express these discrepancies, reflecting this statement back to the patient, and encourage him to elaborate on these statements.
- Whenever possible therapist avoids argumentation because such act often elicits a counter-argument, particularly if the patient is not yet ready to make a change.
- Working within a motivational interviewing framework therapist rolls with resistance, meaning that he or she switches strategies as needed to avoid argumentation, these helps that therapist and patient remain on the same side, rather to be in opposition.
- He or she attempts to support self-efficacy, or the patient's belief in his or her ability to do a specific task, these increase the patient's feelings of hope and optimism that it is possible to make the desired change (Osborne, Raichle, and Jensen, 2006).

By emphasizing empathic listening, frequent patient affirmations, gentle persuasion, and avoidance of argument, significantly reduces patient resistance to clinician-patient interactions and could make treatment more effectiveness, hold patient's satisfaction with the treatment, as well decrease the possibility of relapse (Jensen, 2002). Motivational Interviewing could be defined as "*a client-centred, directive style for enhancing intrinsic motivation to change by exploring and resolving ambivalence*" (Miller and Rollnick, 2002). It evolved from the work of the psychologist Carl Rogers (1959) on the client-centred counselling framework but departs from traditional Rogerian client-centred therapy because it is *focused to the goals*. Motivational interviewing is nonjudgmental, non-confrontational and non-adversarial, where therapist use ability to ask open-ended questions, to provide affirmations, the capacity for *reflective listening*, and the ability to periodically provide summary statements to the client (in Lane and Rollnick, 2009).

Stewart et al. (1995) described another form of *The Patient-Centred Model,* which has origins in the work Carl Rogers and can be also used to emphasizes a collaborative process of provider-patient interaction: developing a common, shared understanding of the problem or illness; addressing the patient's feelings, beliefs, expectations, and concerns, knowing the "whole person" and his family and social context, and collaboratively choosing among options for treatment, behaviour change, and follow up process. These elements reflect a process characterized by partnership, collaboration, and respect, a process that seeks to understand the meaning of the patient's experiences, needs, values, and preferences, and a process that shares control and responsibility for decision making.

As a central concept in chronic illness care and has become a core component of interventions to improve the outcomes for patients with chronic conditions (Bodenheimer, Lorig et al., 2002; Lorig and Holman, 2003) appear also *concept* of *Self-management*. It is broadly defined as all that a patient does to manage her chronic condition, to live her life as fully, and as productively as possible (Bodenheimer, Lorig et al., 2002; Lorig and Holman, 2003). Loring and Holman (2003) described three general domains of Self management: ability to control symptoms and disease activity (*medical management*), ability to carry out every day activities as a partner, parent, worker, also as a holder of other roles (*role management*), and the coping with emotions, positive and negative (*emotional management*). Competence in self-management does not appear overnight, it is process. Hibbard et al. have (2005) described *four stages in development of such patient's capacity*: to be unaware of the important of taking an active role in self management, to be aware, but with low knowledge, skills and confidence, to have knowledge and start to be active, but have limited confidence, and the highest level of self management is considered the phase in which the individual has already adopted new behaviour patterns and acquired confidence in sustained behaviour change.

As many as *40 percent of patients with a chronic illness are in the first two stages of activation*, these patients are less likely to engage in a wide variety of self-management behaviours (Hibbard et al., 2005; Hibbard and Tusler, 2007) *and have poorer health* (Mosen et al., 2007). On the other hand, longitudinal studies have found that patients who progress to a higher stage of patient activation are more likely to adopt self-management behaviours (Hibbard, Mahoney, Stock and Tusler, 2007) and are in better health form.

Self management support is the term of the systematic provision of education and supportive interventions to increase patients' skills and confidence in managing their health problems (Adams, Corrigan and Committee on Identifying Priority Areas for Quality Improvement, 2003). It means next activities:

- Assessment the patient's belief, behaviour, and knowledge;
- Collaborative goal setting;
- Identification of personal barriers and support;
- Skill teaching, including problem-solving to address barriers;
- Increasing access to resources and supports;
- Developing a personal action plan that is based on previous steps (Glasgow et al., 2002; Fisher et al., 2005).

It can be characterized as a process for educating and empowering patients that is quite different from traditional information-focused educational strategies. Management support interventions are often delivered by clinicians or other health care staff within clinical settings, but elements of self-management support may also be delivered in community settings by lay educators, peer counsellors, or other community-based workers (Fisher et al., 2005; Glasgow, Strycker, Toobert, and Eakin, 2000; Lorig and Holman, 2003). Controlled trials of self-management support interventions have produced improvements in clinical outcomes across a number of other chronic conditions (Bodenheimer, Lorig et al., 2002; Lorig and Holman, 2003; Warsi, Wang, LaValley, Avorn, and Solomon, 2004).

Rotter and Kinmonth (2002) identified within self-management support *five effective self-management support interventions*: to hear from a patient perspective; to provide the information that is useful and relevant and check for accuracy; to negotiate a plan and anticipate problems; to offer ongoing monitoring and follow up; to find problems and renegotiate solutions; and to offer an emotional support. Supporting patient autonomy, for example, by offering treatment options in a patient-centred and non-controlling way appears to promote follow-through and successful behaviour change (Williams, McGregor, King, Nelson, and Glasgow, 2005; in Goldstein, DePue, and Kazura, 2009).

CONCLUSION

As benign chronic pain can be treated according to the traditional view of pain with a combination of pharmacological and physical therapies, and sometimes even by surgery, or it can be treated according to the bio-psycho-social approach in an integrated therapeutic manner, it is important to verify which forms of resistances can appear in both forms. A patient's non-adherence to the regimen of prescribed analgesics, sedative, sleeping and other pills is demonstrated through a complete suspension of pills intake, or pills taken as they see fit, taken in quantitative or time limited form or taken in very large amounts.

This is similar to other recommendations by the doctor. For example, a pain patient may not carry out physical exercises; furthermore, he or she could become increasingly physically, mentally and socially inactive. The biomedical view of pain follows from the assumption that every report of pain is directly associated with a specific physical cause and that the extent of pain should be proportional to the amount of detectable tissue damage. Therefore, physicians may spend a great deal of time attempting to establish the link between the pain complaints and the tissue damage, verified through the use of biomedical inquiries. Their expectation is also that once the physical cause has been identified, appropriate treatment (pharmacologically, physiotherapy, surgery) will follow. This standpoint may be appropriate in the case of acute pain, according to Turk and Okifuji (2002), but could be completely unproductive in the case of chronic pain. Let us remember that there may be a patient's reports of pain in the absence of identifiable pathology, and pathology in the absence of pain (see the study by Jensen et al. in 1994, that CT and MRI have shown significant pathology in up to 35 percent of asymptomatic persons).

The problems in treatment occur when the patients' symptoms and illness are not commensurate with the degree of observable pathology. This happens usually after a long process of gathering the laboratory, EMG, CT, and MRI data, and the use of different analgesics, all to little or no effect. Both the doctor and the patient might be frustrated; the first because of the belief that he has exhausted all options, and the patient because despite the torment of tests and the various approaches implemented by the doctor, the pain is still present. The patient has not only lost hope, he/she also presumes that the doctor does not believe him or her anymore.

If such a situation is also accompanied by the doctor's explanation: "It is all in your head!", the patient's distress and doubts grow: "Who is right? Is it the doctor's error or am I imagining the pain?"

Certainly, there are many such cases in the traditional treatment of non-malignant chronic pain. They create anger and mistrust not only in the doctor, but in the health care system as a whole.

Moreover, this incurs substantial costs for the health care budget. A dissatisfied patient begins to pressure the doctor with requirements for new and fresh inquiries, another therapy, evidence of incapacity to work, and finally, also for early retirement.

The patient is not able to understand how it is possible that despite the negative test results and all other medical interventions, he still suffers pain. Therefore, in traditional chronic pain treatment, it is important to focus on interventions which increase patient satisfaction instead of merely pursuing strict adherence to prescribed medication. Appropriate communication between doctor and patient, in which information is exchanged and not simply provided, leads to effective treatment. For example, patients need to know the benefits and side-effects of medication (and conversely, in order to improve adherence, physicians need to know patients' beliefs and attitudes towards medicine taking), but they also need to know what is realistic to expect, to participate in establishing a therapeutic plan and goals, as well as a timeframe to achieve them.

An empathic attitude on the part of the doctor evokes feelings of understanding and support in the patient, and consequently their readiness to take an active role in treatment grows.

The ability of patients to follow treatments in an optimal manner is frequently compromised by a number of barriers. Interventions to promote adherence require several components to target these barriers, and health professionals must follow a systematic process to assess them all. To make this method of practice a reality, the health care provider should have access to specific training in adherence management: about information on adherence; a clinically useful method of using this information and thinking about adherence; behavioural tools for creating or maintaining habits.

It can happen that the pain patient is directed to psychological treatment after the torment of diagnostic procedures and testing of the effects of the various available medical options.

At this point, chronic pain patients might be completely frustrated and embedded in a passive, "sick role". The therapist is confronted with a large number of direct or concealed forms of resistance which need to be discussed openly. What is essential is that feelings of comfort (relaxation training, breathing exercises, and visualization) are aroused in the patient and that his/her confidence increases through the Patient-centred model and the principles of Motivational Interviewing (MI). In this way, the patient later included in Cognitive-Behaviour therapy (CBT) acquires the willingness and ability to make changes.

REFERENCES

Bandura, A., O'Leary, A., Taylor, C. B., Gauthier, J., Gossard, D. (1987). Perceived self-efficacy and pain control: Opioid and nonopioid mechanisms. *Journal of Personality and Social Psychology,* Vol 53 (3), 563-571.

Bandura, A. (1986). *Social foundations of thought and action: A social cognitive theory.* Englewood Cliffs, NJ: Prentice Hall.

Bandura, A.(1994). Self efficacy. In V. S. Ramachaudran (Eds.), *Encyclopedia of human behaviour* (Vol. 4, pp. 71-81). New York: Academic Press.

Bandura, A. (1995). Exercise of personal and collective efficacy in changing societies. (pp.1-45). In A. Bandura (Edit), *Self efficacy in changing societies* (pp.1-45). Cambridge: Cambridge University Press.

Bandura, A.(1997). Self efficacy: the exercise of control. New York: Freeman Publisher.

Broekmans, S. (2011). *Medication adherence in patients with chronic non-malignant pain: an exploratory study.* Leuven: PhD thesis in Biomedical Sciences.

Broekmans, S., Dobbels, F., Milisen, K., Morlion, B., and Vanderschueren, S. (2010). Determinants of medication underuse and medication overuse in patients with chronic non-malignant pain: a multicenter study. *International Journal of Nursing Studies,* 47(11), 1408-1417.

Butow, P. (2012, Avgust 28). The Key to Patient Care and Adherence. Milan: 14 th World Congress on Pain 2012, IASP.

Claxton, A. J., Cramer, J., Pierce, C. (2001). A systematic review of the associations between dose regimens and medication compliance. *Clinical Therapeutics,* 23(8), 1296-1310.

Corrado, P., Griswold, D., and Murray, J. (2012). Medication Adherence and Compliance: Uncontrolled Variables in Psychiatric Clinical Drug Trials. *Advances in Pharmacoepidemiology and Drugs Safety* 1: 107.doi: 10.4172/apds.1000107.

Deci, E. L. and Ryan, R. M. (2000). The "what" and "why" of goal pursuits: Human needs and the self-determination of behaviour. *Psychological Inquiry,* 11, 227-268.

Dunbar-Jacob, J., Schlenk, E. A., Caruthers, D. (2002). Adherence in the Management of Chronic Disorders. In A. J. Christensen and M. H. Antoni (Eds), *Chronic Physical Disorders. Behavioral Medicine's Perspective* (pp. 69-82). Oxford: Blackwell Publishing.

Fernandez, E. and Turk, D. C. (1997). The utility of cognitive coping strategies for altering pain perception meta- analysis. *Pain,* 38, 123-135.

Folkman, S. (1997). Positive psychological states and coping with severe stress. *Social Science and Medicine,* 45 (8), 1207-1221.

Graziottin, A., Gardner-Nix, J., Stumpf, M., and Berliner, M. N. (2011). Opioids: how to improve compliance and adherence. *Pain Practice,* 11 (6), 574-581.

Goldstein, M. G., DePue, J., and Kazura, A. N. (2009). Models of Provider-Patient Interaction and Shared Decision Making. In S. A. Shumaker, J. K. Ockene, and K. A. Riekert (Eds), Handbook of Health Behavior Change, 3th edit (pp.107-125). New York: Springer Publishing Company.

Gonder-Frederick, L., Cox, D. J., Clarke, W. L. (2002). Diabetes. In Christensen, A. J. and Antoni, M. H. (Eds), Chronic Physical Disorders. Behavioral Medicine's Perspective (pp.137-164). Oxford: Blackwell Publishing.

Holroyd, K. A. and French, D. J. (1995). Recent Developments in the Psychological Assessment and Management of Recurrent Headache Disorders. In A. J. Goreczny (Edit.) Handbook of Health and Rahabilitation Psychology (pp. 3- 30). New York: Plenum Press.

Ingledew, D. K., Markland, D. (2008). The role of motives in exercise participation. *Psychology and Health,* 23 (7), 807-828.

Jack, K., Mc Lean, S. M., Moffett, K. J. and Gardiner, E., (2010). Barriers to treatment adherence in physiotherapy outpatient clinics: A systematic review. *Manual Therapy*, 15 (3-2), 220–228.

Jensen, M. P. (2002). Enhancing Motivation to change in Pain Treatment. In D. C. Turk, and R. J. Gatchel (Eds), *Psychological Approaches to Pain Management: A Practitioner's Handbook.* 2 nd edit (pp. 71-93). New York: Guilford Press.

Kerns, R. D., Bayer, A. L., and Findley, J. C. (1999). Motivation and Adherence in the Management of Chronic Pain. In A. R. Block, E. E. Kremer, and E. Fernandez (Eds), *Handbook of Pain Syndromes: Bio psychosocial perspectives* (pp 99-123). Malwah, NJ: Laurence Erlbaum.

Kreitler, S. and Niv, D. (2007). Quality of Life and Coping in Chronic Pain Patients. In S. Kreitler, D. Beltrutti, A. Lamberto, and D. Niv (Eds), *The Handbook of Pain* (pp 77-99). New York: Nova Science Publishers.

Lane, C. A. and Rollnick, S. (2009). Motivational Interviewing. In S. A. Shumaker, J. K. Ockene, and K. A. Riekert (Eds), *Handbook of Health Behavior Change*, 3th edit (pp 151-168). New York: Springer Publishing Company.

Le Resche, L., Von Korff, M. (1999). Epidemiology of Chronic Pain. In A. R. Block, E. E. Kremer, and E. Fernandez (Eds), *Handbook of Pain Syndromes: bio- psychosocial perspectives* (pp. 3-22). Mahwah, NJ: Laurence Erlbaum.

Marchand, S. (2009). *The Phenomenon of Pain.* Seattle: IASP Press.

Merskey, H. (1979). Pain terms: a list with definitions and a note on usage. Recommended by the International Association for the Study of Pain (IASP) Subcommittee on Taxonomy. *Pain,* 6, 249-252.

Michultka, D. M., Blanchard, E. B., Appelbaum, K. A., Jaccard, J., and Dentinger, M. P. (1989). The refractory headache patient: 2 high medication consumption (analgesic rebound) headache. *Behaviour Research and Therapy*, 27, 411-420.

Okifuji, A., Turk, D. C., and Kalauokalani, D. (1999). Clinical Outcome and Economic Evaluation of Multidisciplinary Pain Center. In A. R. Block, E. E. Kremer and E. Fernandez (Eds), *Handbook of Pain Syndromes: biopsychosocial perspectives* (pp. 77-97). Mahwah, NJ: Lawrence Erlbaum.

Osborne, T. L., Raichle, K. A., and Jensen, M. P. (2006). Psychological Interventions for Chronic Pain. *Physical Medicine and Rehabilitation Clinics of North America,* 17, 415-433.

Osterberg, L., and Blaschke, T. (2005). Adherence to Medication. *New England Journal of Medicine,* 353, 487-497.

Parsons, T. (1958). Definitions of health and illness in the light of American values and social structure. In E.G., Jaco (Edit), *Patients, physicians, and illness* (pp. 3-29). New York: Free Press.

Raj, P. (2007). Taxonomy and Classification of Pain. In S. Kreitler, D. Beltrutti, A. Lamberto, and D. Niv (Eds), *The Handbook of Pain* (pp. 41-56). New York: Nova Science Publishers.

Rakovec-Felser, Z. (1997). *Pain as the complex, biopsychosocial phenomenon.* Bolečina kot kompleksen, biopsihosocialen pojav. Ljubljana: Doktorska naloga.

Sabaté, E. (2003). *Adherence to long-term therapies: evidence for action.* Geneve: WHO Report.

Skevington, S. M. (2004). Pain and Symptom Perception. In A. Kaptein and J. Weinman (Edit), *Health Psychology* (pp. 182-207). Malden, Oxford, Carlton: BPS Blackwell.

Smith, C. A., Wallston, K. A., Dwyer, K. A., and Dowdy W. (1997). Beyond good and bad coping: A multidimensional examination of coping with pain in persons with rheumatoid arthritis. *Annals of Behavioural Medicine*, 19 (1), 1-11.

Stewart, A. L., Hays, R. D., and Ware, J. E. (1988). The MOS short form general health survey. Reliability and validity in a patient population. *Medical Care,* 26, 724-735.

Stucky, C. L., Gold, M. S., and Xu Zhang. (2001). Mehanisms of Pain. *PNAS, Proceeding of the National Academy of Science,* USA 98 (21), 11845-11848.

Taylor, E. S. (1995). Health Psychology. 3 th edit. Syngapore: Mc Graw-Hill Book Co.

Turk, D. C., and Rudy, T. E. (1991). Neglected topics in treatment of chronic pain patients-Relapse, noncompliance, and adherence enhancement. *Pain,* 44, 5-28.

Turk, D. C. and Okifuji, A. (2002). Chronic Pain. In A.J. Christensen and M. H. Antoni (Eds), Chronic Physical Disorders. Behavioral Medicine's Perspective (165-190). Oxford: Blackwell Publishing.

Turk, D. C. and Monarch, E. S. (2002). Biopsychosocial Perspective on Chronic Pain.. In D. C. Turk and R. J. Gatchel (Eds), *Psychological Approaches to Pain Management: A Practitioner's Handbook,* 2 nd edit (pp. 3-29). New York: Guilford Press.

Turk, D. C. (2002). A Cognitive-Behavioral Perspective on Treatment of chronic pain patients. In D.C. Turk and R.J. Gatchel (Eds*), Psychological Approach to Pain Management. A Practitioner's Handbook.* 2 nd edit (pp.138-158). New York: Guilford Press.

Turk, D. C. and Okifuji, A. (2003). A cognitive-behavioural approach to pain management. In R. Melzack and P.D. Wall (Eds.), *Handbook of Pain Management: a clinical companion to Wall and Melzack's Textbook of Pain.* 1st edit (pp. 533-541). London: Churchill Livingston.

Turk, D. C. and Melzack, R. (2011). The Measurement of Pain and Assessment of People Experiencing Pain. In D. C. Turk and R. Melzack (Eds.), *Handbook of Pain Assessment* (pp. 3-179). New York: Gulford Press.

Zolnierek, K. B. H., Di Matteo, M. R. (2009). Physician Communication and Patient Adherence to Treatment: A meta analysis. *Medical Care,* 47 (8), 826-834.

INDEX

A

abuse, 67
academic performance, 16
academic success, 45
access, 21, 39, 77, 79
ADHD, 5, 14
adherence to treatment, vii, viii, ix, 1, 3, 14, 18, 19, 31, 32, 41, 42, 49
adjustment, 57, 58
Adolescent Questionnaire, 11
adolescents, 10, 16, 18, 33, 45
adult literacy, 2
adults, 35, 47, 54
adverse effects, 33, 35
adverse event, 26, 67
aetiology, 53, 63
affective disorder, 6
age, 10, 15, 21, 28, 42, 54, 55, 56
aggression, 63
AIDS, 16
alcohol problems, 8
alcoholism, 74
alternative treatments, 37
ambivalence, 75
analgesic, 58, 73, 82
anemia, 3
anger, 56, 63, 78
anticonvulsant, 35
antidepressant(s), 14, 17, 18, 35, 66, 73

anxiety, viii, 3, 43, 51, 53, 56, 61, 63, 67, 69
anxiety disorder, 32, 36, 37, 38, 40, 45, 47
appointments, 32, 69, 72
appraisals, 60, 61, 62
arousal, 61, 64
arthritis, 2
assessment, 12, 24, 73
asymptomatic, 78
attitudes, 17, 23, 34, 60, 68, 79
attribution, viii, 32, 41
authority, 5, 72
autonomy, 77
avoidance, 40, 41, 42, 58, 59, 63, 75
awareness, 55, 75

B

back pain, 53, 54, 58, 63, 64, 65
barriers, 2, 11, 15, 21, 37, 61, 69, 70, 77, 79
base, vii, 1, 34, 35
behavior therapy, 16, 32, 35, 42, 44, 46, 47
behavioral change, 2, 28
behavioral medicine, 45
behaviors, 1, 4, 5, 6, 10, 15, 33, 36, 40, 43
benefits, 21, 25, 28, 33, 68, 73, 79
benign, 53, 65, 66, 77
bias, 4
biofeedback training, 73
biomedical approach, vii, 19
bipolar disorder, 35, 40, 47

birds, 62
blame, 14, 26
blood, 11, 12
blood pressure, 17
brain, 51
brain aneurysm, 51
breast feeding, 10
breathing, 79
Britain, 27

C

campaigns, 21
cancer, 2, 53
carbohydrates, 11
cardiovascular system, 52
caregivers, 38, 39, 40, 42, 68
categorization, 13
causality, 70
causation, viii, 19, 25, 26, 27
central nervous system, 52
cervical cancer, 6
challenges, 45, 61
childhood, 15
children, 14, 33, 40
chronic diseases, 33
chronic illness, 5, 6, 33, 71, 76
chronic recurrent, 53
city, 16
classification, 3, 27, 52
clinical implications, vii
clinical psychology, 18
clinical treatment outcomes, vii
clinical trials, vii, viii, 31, 32
cognition, 29
cognitive theory, 22, 49, 80
cognitive variables, 37
collaboration, 76
colorectal cancer, 6
common sense, 29
communication, 2, 4, 6, 18, 26, 27, 33, 38, 45, 46, 68, 79
communication skills, 5, 28
community, 16, 68, 77
community-based services, 3

comorbidity, 41
compensation, 54, 74
complex interactions, 65
complexity, 26, 27, 33, 51
compliance, 5, 14, 20, 27, 29, 35, 41, 44, 45, 61, 63, 68, 72, 81
complications, 11, 43, 50, 71
computer, 17
conception, 70
conceptualization, 73
concordance, 19, 25, 27, 28, 29
conflict, 35
Congress, 80
conscientiousness, 10
consciousness, 62
consolidation, 73
constipation, 67
consumption, 10, 82
containers, 13
control group, 7, 8, 9
conviction, 61
coping strategies, 24, 57, 58, 59, 60, 66, 81
correlation, viii, 32, 35, 42
cost, 17
cost-benefit analysis, 20
counseling, 2, 9
crowds, 57
CT, 63, 78
cues, 20, 21
culture, 27, 55
cure, 63
curriculum, 47

D

daily living, 56
danger, 52
deficiency, 3
deficit, 16
deinstitutionalization, 36, 38
delirium, 3
demographic characteristics, 56
denial, 35

depression, viii, 3, 10, 14, 32, 34, 35, 38, 39, 41, 42, 45, 52, 56, 58, 61, 62, 63, 67, 68, 69
depth, 38
detectable, 78
developed countries, 33
developing countries, 5
diabetes, 2, 5, 10, 11, 12, 16, 45
diet, 4, 10, 11, 12, 50
disability, 51, 58, 60, 63, 65, 74
discomfort, 52, 56
disease activity, 76
disease progression, 50
diseases, 41
disorder, viii, 3, 16, 31, 34, 35, 40, 41, 43, 45, 52, 60, 65
dissatisfaction, 66
distress, 42, 58, 61, 78
doctors, 2, 40
dosage, 11, 27, 68, 73
dosing, 27, 67
drug abuse, 67
drug resistance, 18
drug treatment, 17, 35, 37
drugs, 37, 73
DSM, 38

E

early retirement, 79
education, 6, 23, 27, 39, 43, 44, 46, 47, 56, 69, 76
educators, 77
EMG, 63, 78
emotional experience, 51
emotional responses, 62, 63
empathy, 75
employers, 63
encouragement, 22, 33, 70
energy, 56, 64
environment, 18, 26, 61
environmental factors, 4, 68
error theory, 26, 27, 29
ethnographic study, 29
etiology, 13

euphoria, 35
Europe, 65
everyday life, 58
evidence, 3, 18, 29, 37, 40, 46, 47, 61, 69, 79, 82
evolution, 34, 43
excitation, 63, 64
exercise, 11, 12, 22, 50, 57, 61, 70, 80
exercise participation, 69, 71, 81
expertise, 28
extraversion, 10

F

faith, 67
families, 35, 40, 44, 47
family environment, 38
family functioning, 38
family members, viii, 6, 32, 38, 39, 40, 42, 63
family relationships, 71
family support, 39, 70
family therapy, 35
fatalism, 59
fear(s), ix, 38, 49, 51, 56, 62, 63, 64, 67
feelings, 24, 56, 59, 63, 73, 75, 76, 79
fibromyalgia, 65
financial, 5, 16, 33, 67, 69
financial instability, 13
flight, 51
food, 10, 11, 12
formation, 6
foundations, 80
France, 7
freedom, 5, 74

G

glucose, 11, 16
goal setting, 77
Great Britain, 27
group treatment, 45
growth, 14
guardian, 12

guidance, 70
guidelines, 15, 46, 73, 75
guilt, 3, 38
guilt feelings, 3

H

HAART, 6, 16
headache, 51, 54, 55, 65, 72, 73, 82
healing, 51, 52, 53, 65
health care, 4, 15, 17, 32, 33, 50, 52, 54, 55, 59, 60, 63, 64, 77, 78, 79
health care costs, 33
health care professionals, 32
health care system, 60, 63, 78
health condition, 52
health education, 22, 24
health locus of control, vii, 19, 20, 22, 30
health problems, 58, 64, 77
health promotion, 21, 33
health psychology, 15
health services, 33
health status, 66
helplessness, 51, 60, 69, 73
hemoglobin, 12
history, viii, 8, 31, 33, 34, 41, 67, 69, 74
HIV, 2, 6, 7, 8, 9, 14, 16
homelessness, vii, viii, 31, 34
homework, 37, 41, 45, 72
hopelessness, 51, 73
hospitalization, vii, viii, 31, 34, 71
hostility, 63
human, 26, 27, 28, 29, 80
hyperactivity, 16
hypertension, 16, 17, 56

I

IASP, 52, 65, 80, 82
identity, 74
impairments, 36
improvements, 39, 43, 77
impulses, 64
incidence, 29, 40, 72

income, 21, 57
indirect effect, 23
individual differences, 50, 72
individuals, 22, 24, 27, 35, 39, 40, 44, 55, 74
infant feeding practices, 15
inferences, 54
information seeking, 57
inhaler, 27
inhibition, 63
initiation, 74
injections, 22
injury(ies), 50, 51, 52, 53, 63, 72
insertion, 47
institutions, 50
insulin, 11, 12
interference, 63
internalization, 63
intervention, viii, 6, 7, 8, 10, 16, 25, 28, 32, 37, 39, 40, 42, 43, 45, 46
intrinsic motivation, 75
investment, 11, 12, 33
irritability, 3, 64
isolation, 56
issues, 4, 25, 33, 36, 43, 65, 73, 74

J

joint pain, 55

L

lack of control, 35
lead, 1, 52, 59, 72
leadership, 69
learning, 22, 43
legs, 51, 52
leisure, 56
life expectancy, 50
lifestyle changes, 4, 5, 71
light, 6, 17, 74, 82
literacy, 10
lithium, 35, 47
litigation, 54, 74

locus, 22, 70
low risk, 5
Luo, 10, 16

M

major depression, 35, 56
majority, vii, 1, 2, 50, 55, 62
malingering, 74
mammography, 6
management, ix, 3, 10, 16, 28, 45, 46, 50, 51, 57, 63, 64, 68, 71, 73, 74, 76, 77, 79
mania, 45
marital status, 35
materials, 6
matter, 50
measurement(s), 3, 4, 10, 12
medical, vii, ix, 1, 2, 3, 6, 13, 15, 18, 19, 20, 26, 28, 29, 35, 36, 44, 45, 49, 52, 53, 66, 68, 76, 79
medical care, 5, 51, 54, 72
medication, vii, 1, 2, 4, 5, 10, 12, 15, 16, 17, 20, 26, 27, 29, 30, 33, 34, 35, 44, 46, 53, 57, 58, 64, 65, 66, 67, 68, 71, 72, 73, 79, 80, 82
medication compliance, 80
medicine, 5, 29, 46, 67, 68, 79
mellitus, 5, 10
memory, 26, 27, 34
MEMS, 9
menarche, 54
mental activity, 15
mental disorder, viii, 32, 34, 36, 40, 43, 45
mental health, vii, viii, 1, 3, 4, 6, 31, 34, 36, 38, 39, 44, 45, 47, 66
mental health professionals, 36
mental illness, 38, 44, 47
mental state, 60
meta-analysis, 15, 16, 17, 18, 37, 47, 66, 83
methodology, vii, 1
methylphenidate, 17
migraine headache, 53
misconceptions, 69
misunderstanding, viii, 31, 41
misuse, 46

modelling, 22
models, vii, ix, 19, 20, 25, 28, 49, 50, 59, 70
morbidity, 4, 14, 56
mortality, 4, 14
motivation, viii, ix, 2, 5, 6, 15, 25, 32, 34, 37, 41, 43, 50, 61, 63, 67, 70, 71, 73, 74
MRI, 63, 78
multidimensional, ix, 49, 52, 71, 82
multiple factors, 33
musculoskeletal system, 52

N

negative effects, 66
negative mood, 56, 63
negative reinforcement, 63
negotiation, 27
neuroleptics, 35
neuropathic pain, 65
neutral, 64
New England, 46, 82
NHS, 19
nonadherence, vii, viii, 31, 33, 34, 35, 36, 41
North America, 65, 82
nurses, 10
nutrition, 12

O

obesity, 10
obstacles, 61, 70
obstructive sleep apnea, 17
occupational therapy, 35
opioids, 60
opportunities, 36, 38
optimism, 75
organ, 52
osteoarthritis, 55
outpatient, 16, 81
outreach, 3

P

pain, vii, ix, 49, 50, 51, 52, 53, 54, 55, 56, 57, 58, 59, 60, 61, 62, 63, 64, 65, 66, 67, 68, 69, 70, 71, 72, 73, 74, 77, 78, 79, 80, 81, 83
pain management, ix, 49, 68, 83
pain perception, 51, 81
pain tolerance, 62
palliative, 58
panic disorder, 36, 44
paranoia, 3
parents, 10
paresthesias, 3
participants, 9, 42, 55
pathology, 78
pathophysiology, 65
pathways, 6
perseverance, 61
personal benefit, 67
personal contact, 57
personal control, 22, 61
personal efficacy, 61
personality, viii, 6, 10, 14, 32, 41, 42, 43, 59
personality disorder, viii, 32, 43
personality traits, 14, 41
persuasion, 22, 75
pharmacological treatment, 72
pharmacotherapy, 50, 73
phobia, 41, 42, 47
physical abuse, 74
physical activity, 6, 11, 57, 69
physical exercise, 72, 78
physical therapy, 73
physicians, 33, 34, 36, 52, 59, 68, 78, 79, 82
placebo, 42
planned behaviour, vii, 19, 20, 23
policy, 27, 34, 46
population, 5, 36, 40, 50, 53, 54, 55, 65, 66, 83
positive feedback, 70
positive reinforcement, 70
positive relationship, 66
preparation, 25
prevention, 3, 33, 39, 43, 50, 73
primacy, 28
principles, ix, 22, 36, 43, 50, 74, 79
probability, 42
problem solving, 39, 59, 77
professionals, vii, viii, 22, 26, 28, 31, 33, 34, 79
prognosis, 5, 13, 67
psychiatric disorders, 3, 36, 73
psychiatric illness, 47
psychiatric patients, 34, 35, 38, 46
psychiatry, 46
psychoeducational approaches, vii, 1
psychoeducational program, 39, 40, 47
psychological approaches, vii, 19
psychological distress, 58, 61
psychological states, 81
psychological well-being, 57, 67
psychologist, 75
psychology, 18
psychopathology, 38
psychosocial dysfunction, 58
psychosocial functioning, 36
psychosocial stress, 67
psychotherapy, viii, 14, 18, 31, 34, 36, 41, 47
psychotropic medications, 10
public health, 33, 36, 50

Q

quality of life, vii, viii, ix, 4, 14, 31, 33, 34, 36, 49, 50, 55, 56, 59, 62, 74
questioning, 67
questionnaire, 10, 42

R

rate of return, 58
reactions, 11, 12, 51
reading, 6
reality, 35, 79
recognition, 27
recommendations, 2, 14, 17, 18, 32, 44, 45, 63, 67, 72, 78

recovery, 37, 40, 46
recreational, 57
regression, 25
regression model, 25
regulations, 70
rehabilitation, 38, 47, 60, 63, 65
rehabilitation program, 39, 70
reinforcement, 29
relapses, 40, 70
relatives, 68, 70
relaxation, 57, 73, 79
relief, 43, 53, 68
religious beliefs, 67
requirements, 2, 79
researchers, 34, 38, 60, 64, 68, 69, 70, 72
resistance, 74, 75, 79
resolution, 35
resources, 60, 77
response, 13, 47, 59, 60, 63
rewards, 71
rheumatoid arthritis, 53, 55, 83
risk(s), 4, 28, 29, 67, 69

S

safety, 14, 29
saliva, 17
schizophrenia, 10, 15, 35, 45, 46
schizophrenic patients, 39, 40
school, 16, 45
sedative(s), 58, 73, 78
self efficacy theory, vii, 19, 20, 22
self-efficacy, 6, 61, 69, 70, 74, 75, 80
self-esteem, 36, 57
self-regulatory model, vii, 19
sensation(s), 51, 52, 56. 59
sensory experience, 62, 63
serotonin, 37, 41
services, 3, 21, 27, 33, 36, 38, 44, 52
severe stress, 81
sex, 54
sexual contact, 57
showing, 42
side effects, 10, 15, 21, 33, 34, 37, 64, 67, 68

signals, 60
signs, 63, 71, 72
skin, 18
sleep disorders, 2, 56
sleeping pills, 73
smoking, 2
smoking cessation, 2
social anxiety, vii, viii, 31, 32, 38, 40, 43, 45
social class, 28
social comparison, 57
social context, 76
social life, 39, 57
social norms, 23
social phobia, viii, 31, 32, 38, 40, 41, 42, 43, 45, 47
social relations, 59
social structure, 82
social support, vii, viii, 31, 33, 35, 58, 69, 70
social support network, 33
society, 39, 50
solution, viii, 32, 43, 68
spinal cord, 63
stabilization, vii, viii, 31, 34
state(s), 24, 32, 33, 35, 39, 59, 62, 64
stigma, 36, 44
stimulant, 14, 16
stimulation, 60, 61
stress, 13, 16, 40, 61
stressors, 61
structure, 33, 36
style, 57, 59, 75
subjective experience, 51, 55
suicide, 57
supervision, 65
surgical intervention, 64
susceptibility, 21
Switzerland, 47
symptoms, viii, 3, 11, 14, 21, 32, 33, 40, 41, 56, 60, 63, 71, 76, 78
syndrome, 39, 40, 53

T

target, 27, 79
techniques, 74
technological advances, 4
tension, 53, 55, 58, 60, 62, 63, 65, 73
tension headache, 53, 55, 63, 65
testing, ix, 49, 79
test-retest reliability, 10
tetanus, 6
therapeutic change, 61
therapeutic goal, 73
therapeutic process, 41, 72, 73
therapeutic relationship, 33
therapist, 17, 41, 43, 73, 74, 75, 79
therapy, viii, 6, 15, 17, 18, 31, 35, 41, 42, 44, 45, 50, 66, 67, 68, 73, 75, 79
thoughts, 58, 62, 70
threats, 4, 61
tin, 51
tissue, 3, 51, 53, 78
training, 5, 6, 10, 28, 39, 65, 79
training programs, 6
traits, 18
transportation, 37, 69
trauma, 52, 53
treatment methods, 65
trial, 7, 8, 9, 17, 18, 41, 44, 45
trigeminal neuralgia, 53
triggers, 51, 52
tuberculosis, 18
type 2 diabetes, 18

U

uniform, 12
United Kingdom (UK), 19, 53
United States (USA), 4, 7, 8, 9, 83
urban youth, 16

V

validation, 30
variables, 4, 5, 6, 37, 50, 71
variations, 6
visualization, 79
vocational rehabilitation, 3
vulnerability, 60

W

weakness, 3, 69
weight loss, 3
well-being, 46, 55, 68
withdrawal, 66
work activities, 51
workers, 77
World Health Organization (WHO), 4, 17, 18, 32, 34, 47, 53, 65, 66, 82
worldwide, 54
worry, 62, 68